Becoming
Teddy Roosevelt

—⊶ ⊱◈⊰ ⊷—

"(W)ell crafted and entertaining. . . These two men genuinely liked, re-spected, and trusted each other, and Andrew Vietze makes us like them, too."
Times Record

"Highly readable and entertaining. . . Vietze's excellent story-telling skills revive the life of a remarkable Mainer who left an indelible mark on his state and the nation."
Working Waterfront

"Vivid and dramatic. . .a fascinating story of a famous American hero and an unassuming Mainer, and how each man positively affected the life and career of the other."
Kennebec Journal

"It's easy to see why the author has won awards for his historical writing. . . .it flows at times like a good novel. . . Becoming Teddy Roosevelt is crucial reading for anyone interested in TR."
Big Sky Journal

"A 'must' for any political or biography collection strong in Presidential histories."
Midwest Book Review

Theodore Roosevelt in 1880

Becoming Teddy Roosevelt

How a Maine Guide Inspired America's 26th President

Andrew Vietze

Down East

Introduction

*"The story of Theodore Roosevelt is the story of a small boy
who read about great men and decided he wanted to be like them."*
—Hermann Hagedorn[1]

I was never all that interested in Theodore Roosevelt. Unlike so many other history buffs, I wasn't captivated by his relentless enthusiasm, his rough-and-ready persona, his bullish pronouncements, or his toothy grin. I figured it was all caricature, and to me he was just another rich, dead president whose background of affluence and privilege had very little in common with mine.

That all changed, though, when I discovered he'd climbed Mount Katahdin. As a park ranger at Baxter State Park, the great wilderness that surrounds Katahdin with a whole universe of woodlands, I was required to read *Legacy of a Lifetime*, by John W. Hakola. The dry old tome tells the rather amazing tale of how Percival Baxter, once governor of Maine, assembled the 200,000-acre park that bears his name over the span of decades, piecing it together like a vast woody mosaic. And in its pages is a short account of the twenty-sixth president's climb up the "Mountain of the People of Maine" back when he was a wheezing, asthmatic Harvard student. His guide was Bill Sewall, a backwoodsman from the tiny upcountry hamlet of Island Falls.

Now, this captured my attention. The appeal was twofold; as a Maine Guide and a ranger I was impressed that Roosevelt was able to summit the peak—an all-day task—in what amounted to bedroom slippers, even though everyone else in his party save his guides turned back. Ever the hungry freelancer, I also figured I could sell the story of TR and Sewall to *Down East*. I've done a lot of work for the Magazine of Maine over the years, and I didn't recall ever seeing word of this tale in recent times.

My editor liked the idea, and off I went, picking up the story's track and following it deep into the North Woods. I found that not only did I like Roosevelt, I liked his larger-than-life guide even better. The more I learned about Bill Sewall's grit and wit, the more I realized I wanted to know more about this man from Maine than I could contain in a mere magazine story. When the article was eventually published, it became apparent that many others wanted to know more, too.

Mine was far from the first account of the unlikely friendship that developed between the two men, but most writers dealt with it in a fairly cursory manner. In the innumerable biographies of the former president, Bill Sewall takes up only a page or two or a handful at best. Writers found him a colorful old character, but they left it at that. Something told me, though, that there was more to the story, that this was a uniquely formative relationship for the quirky young New Yorker.

Or, rather, someone told me—Hermann Hagedorn. A writer and poet who would eventually write several books on Roosevelt and go on to help found the Theodore Roosevelt Association, Hagedorn was TR's official biographer and knew him personally. He got his information from the most primary of sources—Roosevelt's always active mouth. Not long before the former president died in January of 1919, Hagedorn asked him to suggest some other people he should be consulting for his biography. In other words, who best knew Theodore Roosevelt?

Roosevelt sent the writer north to Island Falls, Maine, to see his old friend and guide. Before doing so, TR wrote Sewall to tell him Hagedorn was coming. "There is no one who could more clearly give the account of me, when I was a young man and ever since," Roosevelt said in the letter.[2] "I want you to tell him everything, good, bad and indifferent. Don't spare me the least bit. Give him the very worst side of me you can think of, and the very best side of me that is truthful. I have told Hagedorn that I thought you could possibly come nearer to putting him 'next me' as I was seen by a close friend who worked with me when I had 'bark on' than anyone else could. Tell him about our snow-shoe trips; tell him about the ranch. Tell him how we got Red Finnegan and the two other cattle thieves. Tell him everything."

And Sewall did. In his wry Yankee way, he filled the writer's ear, giving Hagedorn plenty of material for his two seminal biographies of TR—*The Boy's Life of Theodore Roosevelt* and *Theodore Roosevelt in the Badlands*.

Hermann Hagedorn would no doubt be surprised that history hasn't followed Bill Sewall more closely, that it allowed the woodsman to disappear back into the very forests from which he emerged. In an introduction to the book Sewall himself penned about TR, Hagedorn wrote, in his typically garrulous fashion: "Historians, seeking one after the other for centuries to come to explore the mysteries of the paradoxical career of Theodore Roosevelt, will have more to say of William Wingate Sewall than his Maine neighbors or even the statesmen, scientists, and men of letters who drew him into their councils, when the time came for choosing a national memorial to a great President, are likely now to realize."[16]

Strangely, though, they have never had much more to say about Sewall or his role in TR's personal development. (Perhaps they couldn't get through that sentence.) This book is not the definitive book on Theodore Roosevelt's childhood—supremely eminent historians with names like McCullough and Morris have already written those—and makes no stab at that. Rather it's an attempt to answer a simple question: Who was Bill Sewall, and why did what this son of the soil had to say matter to Theodore Roosevelt?

Somehow the counsel of Island Falls's most famous guide has faded with the passage of time. This might be because the very virtues he championed—the importance of character and integrity, the strength of the individual, the richness and beauty of small-town life, the enlightenment that the "academy of nature" can provide—have also diminished in stature in this Information Age.

With Wi-Fi transmitting the ideas of the urban elites to every corner of the country, and children suffering from nature-deficit disorder, we've all become city folk like Roosevelt. In this age of convenience, when we can download whatever nugget of information we want instantly and adjust the climate control in our homes and cars in moments, we've gotten soft and forgotten how to "shift for ourselves." We could all stand for a tramp in the woods again, to feel the restorative value of the outdoors, to learn a little self-sufficiency, to remember that humans may be intellectual animals, but they're still animals.

And we could all use a guide like Bill Sewall.

A Man to Know

As darkness fell on September 7, 1878, Bill Sewall opened the door to find Theodore Roosevelt standing on his porch. Wearing big spectacles and weighing a scant 135 pounds, the Harvard junior looked both boyish and bookish staring up at the tall Maine guide.[1] Sewall had been expecting Roosevelt and his companions—cousins West and Emlen Roosevelt and his friend Will Thompson—and he ushered them into his big, white-clapboarded farmhouse, which sat square in the middle of Island Falls, Maine.

Built just a few years prior, the Sewall House was not only at the geographic center of the tiny community of some 230 souls[2] in the woods of Aroostook County, but was also its social center, and it was ever a busy place. Four Sewalls lived in its seven bedrooms,[3] and they were frequently joined by another resident or two as well as visitors popping in and out, often looking for their mail. This was the town's post office, its only guest house, and arguably its finest house; there was always something in the oven, and visitors were made to feel welcome. The city boy would be swept into a small-town world the likes of which he'd never experienced.

Through TR's bespectacled eyes, Sewall must have been an imposing figure, filling the door frame, six foot four, healthy and strong at thirty-three. The first white child born in the pioneer town of Island Falls, the Maine guide had spent his entire life in the woods.[4] When he shook your hand you knew it—he had bear-sized paws that were strong and calloused. In background and bearing he was very much like the heroic adventurers that Roosevelt had so idolized as a boy. With his red-tinged hair, full beard, and deep gray-blue eyes, he looked like King Olaf, the hero of Longfellow's *Saga of King Olaf*—TR's favorite poem. He was the kind of confident, no-nonsense man you'd follow into battle.

For his part, Bill Sewall had certainly seen more rugged specimens than this aspiring hunter, and he wasn't particularly impressed.[5] The boy in front of him looked like a "thin pale youngster with bad eyes and a weak heart,"[6] he would later write, who would "guffle" and wheeze due to his asthma.[7]

To be fair, Roosevelt was exhausted by the time he reached Island Falls. He had spent the entire day traveling, having left the small train depot at Mattawamkeag,

Maine, at ten that morning. Fifty-eight miles to the north and east of Bangor (itself a good two hundred miles from Boston), the outpost of 356 citizens boasted the last train station on the European and North American line, built eight years prior, and it was as remote as remote got.[8] Step off the platform at Mattawamkeag, and you walked into a frontier as real as the one being opened up out West. Anyone wanting to head into the North Woods to visit Island Falls would make the rest of the journey by buckboard, and it would take the better part of six or seven hours to do it. By the time TR reached the front porch of the Sewall House, he had some miles on him, and despite the excitement and activity swirling inside the house, very shortly after arriving he climbed the stairs to the third floor, settled himself in a field bed, and fell asleep.

Not only had Roosevelt spent a long day traveling, but he wasn't feeling well, in either body or spirit. The guide wasn't far off in his initial assessment of the young man. Roosevelt's heart was, if not weak, at the very least sick. The boy had suffered from a fairly severe case of asthma since he was a toddler, and he had endured an attack earlier in the day. This was before the dawn of inhalers, and these wheezing fits were genuinely menacing, taking a lot out of him. But there was more troubling TR than that.

Seven months earlier Roosevelt's father, Theodore Roosevelt, Sr., a giant in his son's life, had succumbed to a gastrointestinal tumor, and the young "Teedie," as he was called at home, felt the pangs of his passing as others might feel hunger. The two had been particularly close, the senior Roosevelt having been a stabilizing influence on his son, a constant source of strength and counsel. Without him TR felt rudderless, and he'd been despairing for the entire summer. And then, just a few days prior to his leaving for Maine, on a trip that he'd be planning for two years, his best friend, Henry Minot, perhaps the most supportive and sympathetic of his Harvard chums in his time of grief, walked out of his life, too.[9] Minot's father had withdrawn him from Harvard. By the time he arrived in the North Woods, Roosevelt was not only exhausted but bereft. "I feel very sad," he wrote in his diary that day.[10]

Things were a little different the next morning. It would be hard to stay glum at the Sewall House. First, the place was alive with activity—people dropping by, Sewalls setting off for a day in the woods, meals being cooked and served. You couldn't be in your own head for very long. And Bill Sewall's family was a warm and hospitable clan, very attentive to their guests. His father, Levi, had started a tradition of helping and hosting the few visitors who made their way to Island Falls.

The first Sewalls in Aroostook County had had to toil endlessly to create their homestead, and sharing with neighbors and visitors had been necessary for survival. Once they were established in their wilderness settlement, they did everything they could to help those who followed.[11] On the census forms in 1880, the Sewall House was described as a hostelry and Sewall listed his occupation as "hotelkeeper."[12]

But it certainly wasn't the sort of hotel Theodore Roosevelt was used to staying in. More a guest house with six residents, it had an open-door policy for hunters, and it was constantly filled with characters. Bill's two older brothers were frequent visitors and quite a pair. "Sam was a deacon,"[13] Roosevelt would later write. "Dave was *not* a deacon." The loving touch felt throughout the home came courtesy of Bill's mother and his sister Sarah. "Mrs. Sewall, the mother, was a dear old lady," Roosevelt recalled.[14] "And Miss Sewall, the sister, was a most capable manager of the house."

Friends and neighbors came and went from sunup to sundown. Island Falls was a tightly woven community, and the Sewalls were among its most important threads. A local historian, who chronicled the foundings of each municipality in Aroostook County, would report in 1922: "[W]e have visited few towns where there is so general a community of feeling and such a genuine each-help-the-other spirit as in this town of Island Falls. Every man says his neighbor is the best fellow in the world, and I think they all tell the truth."[15]

Roosevelt's two cousins had experienced all this warmth and color before. They had visited a couple of years earlier, having headed north with TR's then tutor, Arthur Cutler, for a hunting trip with Sewall, whom they had found by happy accident.[16] Emlen was a year older than TR. He had a mind for business and was a trusted source of financial wisdom for his younger first cousin. A student at Columbia, West would become the Roosevelt family physician. All were close, and each one seemed to inherit an outdoor gene. Emlen would hunt—and correspond—with Sewall for years. West would go on to co-author a book called *The Out of Door Library* in 1897. The state of Maine was beginning to enjoy a reputation as a wilderness playground by the 1870s, thanks to the writings of Thoreau, the paintings of Frederic Church, and the coming of rail, which opened up the Maine woods as never before. Savvy entrepreneurs in places like Greenville were actively marketing North Woods adventures, publishing Baedekers like John Way's *Guide to Moosehead Lake and Northern Maine* (1874) with its enticing maps, and aiming them squarely at the sports of the eastern cities.

Cutler and the Roosevelt boys were just the sort of men they were targeting, affluent and adventurous. They had already decided on a Maine trip when they ran into an acquaintance of Cutler's at the train station in Boston, who told them the place to go in the North Woods was Bill Sewall's at Island Falls.[17] A quick glance at the map showed Island Falls to be just as northerly and deep in the wilderness as they wanted, and the well-heeled hunters were off.

At the time, the traditions of the Maine Guide were only beginning. As numbers of anglers and hunters from the urban centers of the Northeast began journeying to the North Woods for months at a time, they were eager for the services of men who could take care of them in the wilderness. In an attempt to attract sportsmen from away, the state legislature overturned an 1853 law that had outlawed hunting by nonresidents and passed new rules that allowed both hunting and fishing during the summer.

Bill Sewall had been guiding since he was twelve, and over the years had already developed a reputation as a "man to know."[18] Arthur Cutler and his party stayed with Sewall about three weeks in the summer of 1876, enjoying themselves thoroughly. "I had the whole party to take care of, not to speak of the camp," recalled Sewall. "And altogether I had a pretty busy time and wasn't able to give them as much attention as I wanted, but they got plenty of trout and went home satisfied."[19]

TR had been captivated by the stories he heard from his cousins and his mentor and former tutor Arthur Cutler, and he couldn't wait to make the journey into the Maine woods himself. Arthur Cutler understood Theodore Roosevelt well— he'd been teaching the boy since 1873—and he'd been on prior hunting trips with him and his cousins in the Adirondacks.[20] A recent Harvard grad, Cutler was nine years older than TR, and Roosevelt's father had hired him to help his son get into the prestigious Massachusetts university. Teedie would become the first graduate of the Cutler School for Boys (later the Cutler School), and Cutler continued teaching the sons of America's elite for more than forty years; other famous alumni included J.P. Morgan and Waldorf Astor. He thought Bill Sewall might be a very good influence on the boy. The guide didn't smoke or drink and he was a pious man, reading the Bible daily. He also had a quiet but persistent enthusiasm that matched Roosevelt's own, putting his boots on each day with a zeal to get out and do. Cutler knew instinctively that the youngster he had spent so many hours with over the years would find the guide an appealing character, a Davy Crockett in the flesh, a living Daniel Boone. And he figured Sewall would be the type to help the boy get his head straight with the recent death of his father.

Cutler also understood that, because Roosevelt would probably take to Sewall, he'd likely be eager to please him. But he recognized that TR was more vigorous and capable in his head than he was in his body, so he asked the guide ahead of time to go easy on the kid. "I want you to take that young fellow, Theodore, under your special care," he said. "Be careful of him, see that he doesn't take too hard jaunts and does not do too much. He is not very strong and he has got a great deal of ambition and grit, and if you should take such a tramp as you are in the habit of taking sometimes, and take him with you, you never would know that anything ailed him. If you should ask him if he was having a good time he would tell you he was having a very good time; and even if he was tired he would not tell you so. The first thing you knew he would be down because he would go until he fell."[21]

On Roosevelt's first full day in Island Falls, he arose ready indeed to get going, but this was Sunday, which for TR had always been a day of worship. As the hamlet still had no formal church in 1878, Roosevelt instead took a walk and read his Bible, memorizing the Nineteenth Psalm along the way. Bill Sewall was impressed when he heard about that. "Some folks read the Bible to find an easier way into Heaven . . . ," he observed years later. "Theodore reads it to find the right way and how to pursue it."[22]

That afternoon Roosevelt walked down the road to a Methodist meeting at the local school, a simple, three-story, white-clapboarded structure with twin entrances and a chimney at the back. While he cleaned his spectacles and patiently waited for the service,[23] he brooded about losing his best friend from Harvard. "Thinking about poor Hal Minot has again made me think much and oh so sadly of Father's death," he wrote in his diary that night.[24]

On Monday, the guns came out. Roosevelt had been given his first rifle at fourteen, and he'd done a fair amount of hunting in the backyards of his family's summer homes—and in his travels to the Adirondacks and Egypt, where he'd bagged specimens for his growing natural history collection. But he had a lot to learn compared to the Maine woodsman and he knew it right away.

The young New Yorker spent the day hunting for partridge—commonly known as ruffed grouse. The chickenlike birds were frequently seen along the roadsides of Maine at that time of year, strutting and doing their nervous, hop-skip dance in the underbrush or roosting on a branch, but Roosevelt saw nary a one. His thoughts drifted back to his father.

By Tuesday, he was so busy that he didn't have much time for sad reflection. He paddled downstream to Mattawamkeag Lake in a canoe with Wilmot Dow, Sewall's nephew and fellow guide. The son of Bill's sister Pauline, Will was twenty-three—just four years older than TR—and more of a best friend and peer to Sewall than a nephew. He had learned everything he knew at Sewall's side and soon bested his uncle at most outdoor pursuits—the classic case of the gifted student who outgrows his teacher. Sewall recognized this and was more proud than bothered, calling Dow, "a better guide than I was, better hunter, better fisherman, and the best shot of any man in the country. . . . He was growing into a strong man, a master hand in all the ways of the woodsman."[25]

Sewall, West Roosevelt, and the boys' friend Will Thompson were in a ba-teau, a boat of the sort traditionally used by guides and lumbermen in the Maine woods. With a flat bottom and flared sides, it was more stable than a canoe for standing and pickpoling logs and could transport a large load of gear comfortably.

From Sewall's house it was five miles down the fast water of the Mattawam-keag River to the lake, six square miles of pristine water, forty-seven feet deep and ringed by a forest of virgin spruce and hemlock. Sewall spent a great deal of time on Mattawamkeag and knew it intimately. He frequently paddled it—with guests and without—and he worked its shores for both game and timber. The river drained a vast watershed of swamps and streams, and it often was navigable even when other waterways dried up in the summer sun. The party paddled seven miles down the lake to its outlet where they set up their tents.

Getting out into the woods had a tangible effect on Roosevelt. After days in his funk, he finally "had good fun,"[26] tramping through the woods around the lake and taking potshots at pigeons and ducks. He and Emlen spent the following day doing much the same, shooting at loons and scouring the surrounding wood-lands in search of partridge. They took one—after ten miles of walking—and TR's spirits continued to rise. In his diary that night he mentioned both that he "en-joyed the walk very much" and that he and Emlen are "great companions."[27]

Rain kept the hunters largely in camp for the next few days. They read, cleaned their guns, and played whist and euchre, card games of which Roosevelt was enormously fond, and dined on TR's partridge as well as trout and pickerel, and ducks that someone else shot. TR and Emlen ventured out to spend a few hours at the confluence of the river and the lake, squatting behind bushes in hopes of surprising more ducks, but to no avail. Roosevelt did shoot a night-hawk and even a bat, but that was all. On Saturday he saw a duck, but missed on a long shot.

When the weather finally cleared, TR and Sewall took off into the woods together. Heeding the warnings from Cutler, the woodsman had arranged for his nephew Will Dow to take the other members of the party so he could focus his at-tentions on Theodore. He didn't want the kid to hurt himself. They hiked fifteen miles in search of game, stopping to shoot at a couple of foxes sixty yards away. Roosevelt missed again, and he was beginning to get down on himself about his marksmanship. "I don't think I ever made as many consecutive bad shots as I have this week," he wrote in his diary that night. "I'm disgusted with myself."[28]

He wouldn't get any more practice the next day, another Sunday. After study-ing his Bible in the morning, he spent the afternoon doing housekeeping—rather, camp-keeping—chores. But on Monday, Roosevelt and Sewall set out again. By now the guide had either chosen to ignore the admonitions of TR's tutor or he had seen something in Roosevelt that gave him confidence, because the pair decamped on an extraordinarily ambitious trek—a thirty-mile walk along the Mattawamkeag River. They left at 8 a.m. and hiked for close to eleven hours, stopping only briefly to take lunch. As usual they hunted all the way, but for all his efforts, TR bagged only a single red rabbit, a merganser, and a pair of ruffed grouse.

At nineteen, Roosevelt was an intense, studious, and inquisitive young man, and he took these traits into the woods with him, along with a few habits some folks in Island Falls considered unusual, even odd. (One time, for example, he was so eager to catch a neighbor's rooster that had gotten out of its pen, that he chased it up a ladder to the second story and into a stranger's house, even crawling under the bed for it.[29]) When he wasn't hunting out in the woods, he was collecting. "He had an idea that he was going to be a naturalist," Sewall recalled later, "and used to carry with him a little bottle of arsenic and go around picking up bugs."

TR also had a font of energy as unstoppable as a rushing river—he always needed to be doing something. Sewall was used to clients traveling up to the North Woods to do some hunting and fishing, but they typically comported themselves as if they were on vacation, which translated to an easy pace and ample down time—as much relaxation as adventure. Young Roosevelt wanted none of that. On a few occasions, the guide suggested they pause and drop a line for trout, but TR declined. "Theodore was never very fond of that," Sewall remembered. "Somehow he didn't like to sit still for so long."[30]

They walked for hours and talked for hours, and in the woods around Mattawamkeag Lake Bill Sewall found his impression of Theodore Roosevelt changing. He'd kept a close eye on the boy since he'd arrived, just as the tutor had asked him to. "I did watch him carefully," Sewall would recall later. "He took a lot of watching. Yes, a lot of watching." And in doing so, the woodsman found that at least one of Cutler's observations was true: "He'd never quit."[31]

But he didn't find the bespectacled city boy to be as soft as he expected. "He wasn't such a weakling as Cutler tried to make out," Sewall explained. "We traveled twenty-five miles afoot one day on that first visit of his, which I maintain was a good fair walk for any common man."[32]

Unlikely a pair as they may have been—the one a privileged, highly educated boy from New York City, the other a pioneer lumberman from the frontier—they bonded quickly. Arthur Cutler had known this would happen, and in fact it wasn't all that uncommon for clients to bond with their guides. The woods have a way of making unusual allies—it's usually love or hate because of the forced intimacy of close quarters and the teamwork required in remote settings.

But both Sewall and Roosevelt found that despite their many differences, there were more than a few similarities in their lives. Both had endured sickly childhoods. Both had a deep admiration for epic poems and adventure literature. Sewall was as much a fan of Sir Walter Scott and Henry Wadsworth Longfellow as Roosevelt was, and he was prone to lengthy recitations while he hunted (and even as he got dressed in the morning, for that matter).[33] Even more central to their bonding, though, they discovered that both were constantly astonished by the poetry of the natural world. Not everyone who ventures into the woods can appreciate its subtleties.

The one complemented the other in an uncanny way. Sewall was an unusual backwoodsman—few if any of his logging peers could cite *Marmion* line for line, or would have been sensitive enough to reveal it if they could. Roosevelt was just as unlikely as a city boy—raised in the height of luxury, he was as comfortable sleeping on pine boughs in a canvas tent as he was on a feather bed in his Manhattan brownstone. Few men, backwoods bred or not, could match his zeal for the natural world.

"He was different from anybody I had ever met," wrote Sewall. "Of course he did not understand the woods, but on every other subject he was posted." The guide was clearly taken with his new friend. "Especially, he was fair minded. He and I agreed in our ideas of fair play and right and wrong. Besides, he was always good-natured and full of fun. We hitched well, somehow or other, from the start."[34]

Now that he had a better sense of the young man, Sewall let him go out with Will Dow over the next few days. West Roosevelt went with them. Taking the canoe to the upper end of the lake in search of ducks, they shot through the marshy area there with "indifferent success," as TR put it in his diary. That meant they got a dipper duck and a wood duck, and when it came time to pull out and make camp they had a very "frugal" dinner.[35]

The next morning they got up at four and resumed their hunt before the sun rose. Later in the day, TR took a ten-mile walk with Dow, shooting just four times. Even so, he came home with another merganser and three grouse—and a fondness for hiking in moccasins, which was something new for him.

He was at it again the next day, logging another fifteen miles in the woods, three of which were through a tangle of alders that made for terrain "about as difficult as any I have ever been through."[36] He took a spruce partridge in a cedar swamp and another partridge on a hemlock ridge.

Perhaps because he was busy, perhaps because he was making new friends, perhaps because living outdoors fed something in him, Roosevelt began to move past the grief he had carried with him from home. References to his sadness became fewer in his diary, and he certainly didn't voice any of his troubles. "In their company I would have been ashamed to complain," he'd say later.[37] The playful spirit of his guides didn't hurt. On one occasion they propped up a dummy bird for the eager TR to get a bead on. "Was nicely sold by the boys with a dead duck placed in a life like attitude," he duly recorded in his diary.[38]

If he was reflective at all during the latter part of this Maine sojourn, it was not about the death that had so weighed on him just before his arrival, but about how much he loved being in the woods. "The leaves are now beginning to turn and the woods are perfectly beautiful," he wrote. "I have enjoyed this week very much; the trip so far has been a great success."[39]

After spending two weeks in the bush, the party broke camp and started back to Island Falls on September 23. They piled into the boats, and Sewall paddled, Dow and TR rowed, Will Thompson trolled, and West and Emlen Roosevelt watched from the bow for ducks and loons. When they landed, TR spent the remainder of the day in the woods hunting with his cousin West.

During the next two days, Dow took Roosevelt out alone, first on a twenty-five-mile romp and then on a buckboard ride, searching for game all the while. During the course of these jaunts, TR bagged seven more grouse. Even though his tally of kills was lengthy by today's standards—twenty-four animals over two weeks—he considered the hunting aspect of the trip fairly unsuccessful. "I have had wonderfully bad luck as regards shooting, finding very little game," he wrote in his diary. "But nevertheless have enjoyed the trip greatly. There has been absolutely no disagreement between any members of the party."[40]

On Thursday, September 26, Theodore Roosevelt and his new friends parted. TR and his cousins took a buckboard back to Mattawamkeag station and boarded the night train for Boston. Roosevelt would return to Cambridge to resume his studies at Harvard, his comrades would continue on to New York.

Bill Sewall and Wilmot Dow went back to their normal routines in Island Falls, turning again to the projects that usually occupied them in the fall. They would have harvested their gardens, begun to ready their houses for the weather ahead, prepared for another season of cutting trees, and gotten back into the affairs of the town they were building out in the woods.

And they discussed the weeks past, unaware of their significance and the future they would portend. "At the end of the week I told Dow that I had got a different fellow to guide from what I had ever seen before," Sewall recalled. "I had never seen anybody that was like him, and I have held that opinion ever since."[41]

The Nature of New York

Maine wasn't new to Theodore Roosevelt when he first visited Island Falls in 1878. He had made a fateful trip to the North Woods once before, a visit that was both an epiphany for him and something he'd just as soon have forgotten. Six years earlier, when he was fourteen, he'd had a serious asthma attack at his New York home, and his parents thought the crisp mountain air of Maine would do him good. They sent him off to Moosehead Lake.

At the time the Greenville area was enjoying a reputation as a back-of-beyond sort of paradise. The Kineo House had opened in 1848, James Russell Lowell had explored the region in his 1853 *Moosehead Journal*, and Thoreau had brought it wide attention with the publication of *The Maine Woods* in 1864. By the time Roosevelt was a teenager, the little resort town boasted several hotels, steamships to get people about the great lake, and plenty of cool pine air.

TR's mother and father bundled him off to the train station in late summer, and he made his way north to Maine on his own, transferring to a stagecoach for the last part of the journey. Aboard, he found a pair of boys close to his own age. "I have no doubt they were good-hearted boys, but they were boys," TR would write later. "They found that I was a fore-ordained and predestined victim and industriously proceeded to make life miserable for me."[1]

This situation said a lot about Theodore Roosevelt. He was a peculiar child, extremely bright and sensitive, but small, weak, and coddled to a certain extent—a perfect target for bullies. Because of his asthma, his parents, Martha and Theodore Roosevelt, Sr., were very protective of him. In the past, he'd seldom found himself in uncontrolled situations, and when he had, one of his close cousins or his brother, Elliott—bigger and stronger, though younger—would often step in to defend him.

But Roosevelt was alone on this trip, so he was forced to show for himself. He made a valiant stand but soon found that either of those two boys could take him easily. They would, as he put it, "handle me so as not to hurt me much and yet to prevent my doing any damage whatsoever in return."[2] The real hurt, though, was inside, contusions to the pride—the pair were free to torment him at will, and there wasn't much he could do about it.

Roosevelt reached a decision during that hellish stage ride, a decision that would ultimately change his entire life. "The experience taught me what probably no amount of good advice could have taught me," he later explained. "I made up my mind that I must try to learn so that I would not again be put in such a helpless position."[3] He would embark on a training regimen to build his body—and make it equal to his mind. He would learn to fight. He'd shape himself into the kind of man he wanted to be.

His parents were only too happy to help, especially his father, a big, powerful champion of the manly pursuits. The Roosevelts both doted on their children. Little "Teedie" was the second of four. His sister Anna ("Bamie," from *bambino*) was three years older, and seemed so beyond her years that TR considered her a de facto adult and allied himself with his younger brother Elliott ("Nell" or "Ellie") and sister Corinne ("Conie") as the kids.

A precocious, inquisitive child, TR had from the earliest age shown a boundless interest in both the outdoors and the pioneers and adventurers who journeyed into uncharted territories. This was unusual since he came into the world in as urban a setting as could be found in mid–nineteenth-century America, born in an upstairs bedroom in the family's four-story house on East 20th Street, just around the corner from busy Broadway in New York City. The Roosevelts' roots had grown right through the pavement and deep into the ground of Manhattan. Little Teedie was the seventh generation to live on that island since Klaes Martensen van Roosevelt arrived in New Amsterdam about 1644.[4]

When he was still a toddler, Roosevelt was paging through David Livingston's *Missionary Travels in South Africa* and studying it with fascination. When other boys were playing marbles and rolling hoops, he was upstairs in his room with a book in his lap or on his belly in the family's small yard watching a colony of ants. As soon as he could read, he began to pick out titles about natural history, and he read voraciously. He was a gifted learner and had the ability to commit to memory things that he'd read only once. He also had a sense of adventure at a very early age, which would take him right out over the edge, quite literally. There was the day a neighbor spied him dangling out a second-story window. As his mother ran to his rescue, she called out to the woman: "If the Lord had not taken care of Theodore, he would have been killed long ago."[5]

Though he was living in one of the world's largest cities, the little Knickerbocker had several windows on the furry and the leafy. New York in the 1860s was hardly the same metropolis it is today—the buildings were not as tall, and there was still a great deal of greenery to be found. A room on the third floor of the Roosevelt home had been converted into a porch. Gazing down from there, the Roosevelt siblings could peer into one of the city's biggest gardens—that of the Goelet mansion on Nineteenth Street—where exotic birds wandered with clipped wings. Next door lived their Uncle Robert Roosevelt, the family raconteur, and his wife, Aunt Lizzie, who kept a houseful of animals. At any given time, their resident menagerie might include white peacocks and pheasants and even a monkey and a cow. Teedie spent hours and days running back and forth between their houses.

Where his aunt and uncle's home was a chaotic mess, the house presided over by his father was serious and formal. In the parlor there was a woodcut of a hunting scene at which Teedie could occasionally be found staring. It depicted a hunter tracking a herd of chamois near a small mountain. Like his siblings, TR worried for one small antelope in particular, afraid that it might be killed by the hunter.

As a boy TR would wander into what passed for the wilds of Manhattan looking for more lively animals—in Madison Square or the new Central Park—and then try to bring them home with him. Families of gray squirrels, woodchucks, and mice all made it into 28 East Twentieth Street so that Teedie could study them. He'd feed the baby squirrels with a syringe filled with milk, and tuck his latest mouse into a flower pot. His parents got used to finding rodents in the icebox and snapping turtles in the yard. In 1873, while living with a host family in Dresden, Germany, during his second trip to Europe, TR would stuff snakes and hedgehogs into his bureau drawers.

The growing boy's interest in nature was indulged to the fullest during summers, when the family would relocate to "the country." Typically they spent the warm-weather months on Long Island, renting several cottages on the shore before settling on a favorite one at Oyster Bay. This was where TR felt most at home. "We children, of course, loved the country beyond anything," he'd write later. "We disliked the city. We were always wildly eager to get to the country when spring came, and very sad when in the late fall the family moved back to town."[6]

Teedie and Ellie and Conie spent these idyllic days hunting frogs, building teepees, and painting themselves with poke-cherry juice to play Indians. Time at Oyster Bay provided Roosevelt with hours of "ornithological enjoyment and reptilian rapture,"[7] as he called it once in a letter to his sister Bamie.

Their father loved to ride, and the kids learned rudimentary horsemanship on their own mount, a Shetland pony named General Grant. With an ocean out one door and the woods out another, these summers were full of magic for the imaginative naturalist, who would happily take off by himself, traipsing around outside with his face in the bushes or down close to the grass. This intensity didn't go unnoticed by the family staff—the Roosevelts brought their usual retinue of servants. The driver who used to whisk the family around

Long Island was intrigued by the child: "He was a reg'lar boy. Always outdoors, climbin' trees, a-goin' birdnestin.' I remember him particular, because he had queer things alive in his pockets. Sometimes it was even a snake."[8]

TR could find things to wonder about even on the streets of New York. When he was still a young boy, Roosevelt's mother sent him to the market around the corner on busy Broadway, but he was stopped in his tracks by a dead seal laid out on a piece of wood. "That seal filled me with every possible feeling of romance and adventure,"[9] he'd later explain.

Day after day the budding naturalist returned to the seal to study it and measure it and write data down in a little notebook. After discovery, for Roosevelt, came the desire to understand his findings, and then to share that understanding with the world. The little blank book of his nature study wasn't blank for long, and the boy toted it with him wherever he went, cataloging what he'd seen. By the age of nine, TR was beginning to write about his discoveries in a more formal way, penning a "Natural History on Insects," and he knew what he was doing, prefacing the essay: "All these insects are native of North America. Most of the insects are not in other books."[10]

The seal skull became the first item in the collection of the "Roosevelt Museum of Natural History," a homespun institution TR founded with two of his cousins—they even had pink Roosevelt Museum labels printed up for their specimens. The boys, with Teedie far out front, would eventually add hundreds of specimens to their museum.

The collection TR accumulated may have started as child's play but it grew into something valuable—in 1871 the American Museum of Natural History, founded just three years earlier, noted in its records that it acquired a turtle, a bat, a red squirrel skull, several birds eggs, and more from Mr. Theodore Roosevelt, Jr. His specimens made it into the Smithsonian as well.

Theodore Roosevelt's outsized interest in the outdoors was something that he had in common with his father. Theodore Roosevelt, Sr. was a trustee of the new American Museum of Natural History and had access to its treasures—both archival and intellectual. This meant that TR could study taxidermy with the top authorities in the field, men such as John G. Bell, who accompanied Audubon when he traveled west. The elder Roosevelt also took his extended family on trips to the Adirondacks and the White Mountains of New Hampshire to play in "the bush." He'd climb trees with his children and get down on his knees and wrestle with them.

The man of the house at 28 East Twentieth Street and his wife were a study in contrasts—he was large, robust, and rather vigorous; she was petite, and her health would turn sour frequently enough that she was commonly described as sickly. (Little Teedie would tell friends in his letters that his health was good but his mother "continues an invalid."[11]) Mr. Roosevelt was adamantly pro Union, a northern abolitionist through and through (as his son would be); his wife was a Southern belle from slave-owning stock, and several members of her family fought as Confederate soldiers. For all their differences, though, they complemented one another when it came to child rearing. Both doted on their children, spending as much time with them as they could. Theodore Sr. was described by TR's brother as an adult who never forgot he was once a child,[12] and he was actively involved with his children in a way that most of his peers would never dream of.

Of course, he could afford to be—he had the advantage of great wealth, inheriting a massive fortune and a prominent position in the family's import-export business. But his real passion was philanthropy, and he became famous as a New York man-about-town, helping to found many of the city's great institutions, not just the American Museum of Natural History but also the New York Orthopedic Hospital.

Again, in contrast to many of his peers, he poured much of his time into charitable social-service work. He helped the families of Civil War soldiers get monies from their loved ones at war; he taught a mission class; and he worked with the Newsboys' Lodging-House, "and in the night schools and in getting children off the streets and out on the farms in the West," according to TR.[13]

He was used to helping children who needed helping—in his own household he had three who needed him, including two who needed him badly. His oldest, Anna, had an affliction called Pott's Disease, which made her bones soft. This gave her a stooped, almost elderly posture from a very young age. Theodore Sr. developed a particularly close relationship to her, often spending Saturdays with her alone.

The doctor who helped the family with their eldest child's spine trouble preached physicality, believing people would feel better if they were more active. TR would take to this philosophy himself, but it was difficult because he had been having asthma attacks—and severe ones—since he was just three years old. These frightening spasms limited what he could do and, along with other chronic stomach problems and a predilection for colds, fevers, and other childhood ailments, cast a pall over his life—and his household—until he went off to college.

His attacks usually came at night, and it was often his father who came to his rescue, whisking him off for carriage rides through the sleeping city, walks in the winter streets, and even trips to distant destinations thought to be salubrious. He rented houses in Dobbs Ferry on the Hudson, in Madison, New Jersey, and even in the countryside outside of Vienna. For TR this special treatment must have made his father seem all the more heroic. And though he was obviously distressed about his health, the boy greatly enjoyed these getaways with his father, and ironically they were the basis of some of the fondest memories of his life. He not only loved his father but he admired him greatly, later referring to him as "the best man I ever knew."[14]

Theodore Roosevelt, Sr. set high standards for himself, and he expected much of his children. "He would not tolerate in us children selfishness or cruelty, idleness, cowardice, or untruthfulness," according to his eldest son.[15] He was stern and a disciplinarian, but at the same time never held back with the love and praise. "He had a great zeal for life—I never knew any one who got greater joy out of living than did my father, or any one who more whole-heartedly performed his every duty."[16]

Just as he held his father in the highest esteem, TR was unusually close to his mother, Martha Bulloch Roosevelt, "Mittie" to her friends. An "unreconstructed"[17] Southern belle, Mittie lavished affection on her children to the point of indulging them. Small, dark haired, beautiful, and gracious by all accounts, she was also patient, which she would have had to be with her oldest boy, especially when he would do things like ask God to "grind the Southern troops to powder,"[18] while saying his prayers one evening during the Civil War.

From his mother Roosevelt inherited his love of adventure tales. She spent countless hours reading him stories of larger-than-life men and feats of heroism, both fiction and nonfiction, books about knights and sailors and soldiers. When he could read on his own he made his way through the family library, devouring such stories as *The Leatherstocking Tales* and *The Rifle Rangers* along with his natural histories. He'd anxiously await the arrival of *Our Young Folks*, a monthly reader that even into adulthood he considered the "very best magazine in the world."[19] Published from 1865 to 1873, *Our Young Folks* was filled with stories by Roosevelt favorites like Mayne Reid and many of the biggest writers of the day, from Harriet Beecher Stowe to Celia Thaxter and Henry Wadsworth Longfellow. Roosevelt later insisted he took its lessons of "manliness, decency, and good conduct" more seriously than what he learned in school, long believing the periodical taught him "much more than any of my textbooks."[20]

Part of this fascination with brave and rugged men no doubt had to do with the powerlessness he felt due to his slight size and chronic asthma. It was also likely due to the wide-eyed wonder he had for his strong and confident father. His mother added to the mix by telling him tales of the feats of bravery performed by his own relations during the Civil War. His uncle Irvine Bulloch, for example, had fired the last gun discharged from the Confederate raider *Alabama* in the disastrous fight with the USS *Kearsarge*. All of these influences contributed to what psychologists today would call a serious case of hero worship.

Roosevelt's "great admiration for men who were fearless" and his even greater desire "to be like them"[21] were behind his growing urge to remake himself. He didn't want to be confined to the sickroom, he didn't want to be afraid of the bigger boys, and he didn't want to be so shy. In later years he often referred to an incident in Frederick Marryat's *Mr. Midshipman Easy* where a sea captain on a British man-of-war is counseling a sailor who is struggling with his fears. The captain tells him that he, too, used to be afraid heading into action, but made up his mind to act unafraid. Despite how he felt inside, he would give the outward appearance of courage—and after a while that was how he actually felt. It was a lesson that stuck in TR's mind—whatever circumstances he confronted he was determined to act courageous.

When he was bested by the bullies on the stagecoach ride in Maine, he was more than hurt or annoyed: he was disappointed in himself. And he resolved to rectify that. His fourteenth year was a big one for Theodore Roosevelt. A number of changes occurred that helped to propel him toward manhood. He made the pivotal decision to build his strength and learn to fight. And at about the same time his father gave him two gifts that changed his life—spectacles and a gun.

Pine Tree Pioneers

I f pioneers and outdoorsmen and men of action were what interested Theodore Roosevelt, he certainly found one in Bill Sewall. The woodsman often referred to his hometown as "the settlement" and the people of Island Falls as "settlers,"[1] and that's essentially what they were. In the mid-nineteenth century the northern third of Maine still had pockets as raw and primitive as the lands being opened up west of the Missouri, and the resourceful individuals who carved out communities in them—men and women like Sewall's parents, Levi and Rebecca—were just as much pioneers as the homesteaders who were heading out West into the Minnesota Territory or onto the Oregon Trail.

Island Falls sits in the southern corner of Aroostook County, a vast region that makes up 20 percent of Maine—large enough to swallow the combined states of Connecticut and Rhode Island. This was the land of the famous Allagash wilderness, and close to 90 percent of its terrain was covered in boreal forest. To the north, east, or west, stood unbroken woods.

When Maine won its statehood from Massachusetts in 1820, much of Aroostook initially remained in the possession of the Commonwealth. The two states had divided the northern half of the more than eight million acres of woodland north of Bangor using a chessboard pattern, with one state owning one township and the other owning the next. At the time, most of this massive area had yet to be formally surveyed, and it must have seemed a fair compromise, allowing both states to access the rich resource of woodlands.

The border to the north of Aroostook, however, was a source of dispute. The Treaty of Paris, which ended the hostilities between the British and the Americans in 1783, had drawn the boundary lines with all the precision of a kindergartner's crayon. The language in the treaty specified that the eastern boundary would be fixed at the source of the St. Croix River. From there, the line would extend "north to the aforesaid highlands,"[2] but no one was quite sure which highlands were *the* highlands, those dividing the watersheds of the Penobscot and St. John rivers or the ones between the St. John and the St. Lawrence. For that matter, no one could be quite sure even where the St. Croix got its start.

None of this mattered until loggers started demonstrating that money did indeed grow on trees. When lumbermen began felling timber in the St. John area and shipping it out—at a handsome profit—the precise location of the international boundary soon became of utmost importance to both countries.

At the time, there were few roads through these vast woods. Most of the early travelers kept to the waterways or used trails trampled by the feet of game and the Natives who followed them. By the late 1820s, communities were just starting to blossom around Houlton and Madawaska, where Acadians had arrived from New Brunswick via the St. John River. A few corduroy tote roads stretched from Houlton to Woodstock and a trail headed south from Houlton, but no formal highways had been built in this part of Maine until the federal government decided it needed to make its presence felt in the northern part of the state. British surveyors, it seems, had been seen sniffing around in The County.

According to reports, these English gentlemen were "appalled by" the "insularity and wilderness character"[3] of these North Woods. This was the last frontier of New England, a place where stands of spruce stood majestic and tall, never touched by an ax or blade. The survey party reported back that the Aroostook territory was "one mass of dark and gloomy forest to the utmost limits of sight."[4] They were not blind to the financial potential of the place, however. They wanted—or rather their Canadian counterparts wanted—to raze this impenetrable forest and ship it out.

Logging companies from New Brunswick, Canada, were already doing so, shipping timber down the St. John, which flows north into Canada, to mills in New Brunswick. Maine men were doing the same thing, cutting and driving logs down to Bangor on the Penobscot River, but they were considered trespassers by the Canadian government and were occasionally arrested. The two groups of lumbermen argued over territory and repeatedly harassed one another. When they resorted to sabotage, the situation started to get ugly. With millions of dollars at stake, neither side—nor either country—wanted to back down.

The U.S. and the British, squabbling like siblings, looked to outside arbitration for help resolving the matter, and in 1827 King William I of the Netherlands agreed to examine their claims. Neither country was happy with his rather unimaginative decision, which split the disputed territory roughly in half, north and south.

By 1828 the United States government had decided to send troops north to protect American interests, and a garrison was established at Houlton. There was no efficient way to move men or supplies to the region, and the next year the feds began to build what became known as the Military Road, between Lincoln and Mattawamkeag, extending it to Houlton in 1830. Later called simply the Aroostook Road, it would remain the principal thoroughfare into Aroostook County until 1871.

As the timber-cutting disputes grew increasingly tense, militias began to form in the towns of Aroostook and men from other parts of Maine began to march up the new road to Houlton. The blockhouses of Fort Fairfield and Fort Kent were built, and eleven companies of soldiers settled in to see what happened. On the other side of the invisible boundary, regiments of the royal artillery were mustering in Woodstock, across the border from Houlton, as well as in other New Brunswick communities. Responding to this threat, the Maine legislature authorized the mobilization of ten thousand more troops from the state militia, and the U.S. Congress offered up an additional fifty thousand men. Soon troops on both side were staring down their sights at one another.

U.S. General Winfield Scott and Maine governor John Fairfield met with Sir John Harvey, the governor of New Brunswick, to come up with terms, and on March 25, 1839, they agreed to an armistice before any shots were fired. The Webster-Ashburton treaty would follow in 1842, fixing the boundary where it sits today and officially concluding what became known as the Bloodless Aroostook War or the more colorful Pork and Beans War.

The escalating tensions and subsequent diplomacy had captured the attention of Mainers all across the state, of course, and some of them saw the potential of the vast undeveloped country along the new Aroostook Road. Like a toy another child is playing with, these lands all of a sudden seemed more desirable than what many had right in their own backyards. Pioneer families began to venture north. Among them was Levi Sewall from the Farmington branch of a sizable southern Maine family. Levi's father, Samuel, had been born in 1764 in the Bath area, and sired eleven children. He was among a fourth generation of New England Sewalls who traced their lineage back to John Sewall, who had emigrated to Newbury, Massachusetts, from Baddesley, England, in the seventeenth century. By the time of Levi's birth, circa 1800, there were Sewalls all over Maine. (Several Sewalls would rise to prominence in Maine and the nation, becoming a vice presidential candidate, a speaker of the Maine house, and governor of the state. Much earlier, one had even presided over the Salem witch trials.)[5]

Few Sewalls had reached Aroostook County, however, simply because there were few people at all in Maine's most northerly shire. The County itself (it's so big that no one challenges the inclusion of the defining article) had just incorporated in 1839, a year or two before Levi Sewall made his way north to hew the town of Island Falls out of its southern reaches. The population density of Aroostook is eleven people per square mile *today*; in the 1840s there were a scant

9,413 people in all of its 6,672 square miles.[6] Most of these hardy folks lived in communities along its northern and eastern edges. Huge woodlands, chains of lakes, and north-flowing rivers dominated its center.

By the 1840s there were still fewer than a dozen formally incorporated municipalities in The County. Townships, land grants, places with names like "Letter G," and a handful of households dotted the remainder of the landscape. This was wild country.

In 1838, Dr. Ezekiel Holmes, a state agriculturalist, did a survey of Aroostook, traveling up the Penobscot and Seboeis rivers and returning via the still unfinished Aroostook Road. His findings ended up in a pamphlet[7] that the state land commissioners distributed to encourage settlement of northern Maine. In those pages, he poses a rhetorical question:

> Should you advise me to go to the Aroostook? Before answering I would ask, Who are you?
>
> If you are already well situated—have a good farm—live in a pleasant neighborhood and are blessed with the common goods and chattels necessary for well being and happiness of your family, stay where you are, go neither east nor west.
>
> Are you a man of feeble health, with little capital, unable to undergo the severe toils of subduing the forest, and unable to hire? It would not be advisable for you to go there.
>
> Are you idle, lazy, shiftless, and vicious? Go not thither. If you cannot reform, better to stay where alms houses and prisons are more abundant to administer to your necessities.
>
> Are you in straitened circumstances but in good health, with a robust and hardy family of children to assist you? Go to the Aroostook!

He might as well have been talking directly to Levi Sewall.

The Farmington cobbler found his way to the North Woods by accident—or rather, as the result of an accident. He was a native of the coast, born in Phippsburg in 1800, and spent much of his early career making shoes. He married Rebecca Alexander, a tailoress from nearby Harpswell, one year younger than he. The couple soon had six children to feed and keep in dresses and shoes. Sewall did his best, working at the shoemaker's trade for twenty years, but as he got older he found the job too sedentary. He wanted more challenging activity and hired on at a machine shop.

Levi Sewall so enjoyed his new position at a woolen company that he invested not only his labor but his entire savings in the business. A few years later, when the company's mill burned—just a day after their insurance ran out—Sewall and many others were left penniless.

For the next three years, Sewall struggled to provide for his family. Rebecca had a sister in Illinois who was pressuring the couple to join her there. Levi ultimately resigned himself to a move and was considering her offer.[8]

And then he met Jonas Drury.

Drury was a schoolteacher who had recently traveled all the way up to Patten and Houlton on business for the state. On his way between those two communities, he had paused to marvel at a pretty little island in a fast stretch of the West Branch of the Mattawamkeag River, and he was effusive in his praise of the spot when he met Levi Sewall, telling him all about the waterway, its cascades, and the bountiful forest it wended through. These undisturbed woods would make a fine spot for a home, he assured Sewall. The landscape sounded beautiful, but what really grabbed the machinist's attention was Drury's description of the falls, which he knew could provide the water power for industry. Better still, the land could be had cheaply. Being a practical man, Levi figured if he had to move anyway, it would be less expensive to venture north in Maine than it would be to move his family out West.

Eager to have a look at once, he found a few others who were interested in making a scouting trip. In June 1842, the group traveled up the new Aroostook Road. When they asked in the small town of Patten whether anyone could tell them how to get to the island and falls in the Mattawamkeag River, they were greeted with blank stares—no one knew the place. Eventually they found one man who might have heard of it; he gave them approximate directions, and they headed off through the woods. Taking an easterly course, they hit Fish Stream and followed it downstream to the Mattawamkeag.

The group bushwhacked along the river for awhile but couldn't be sure where they were or whether they had gone too far past the falls, so they made camp for the night. Levi rose early the next day, and "in the profound stillness of the morning"[9] he heard the falls. After reaching the island and the falls and exploring the woodlands and the intervales, Sewall decided the schoolteacher had been right. Another member of the party, Jesse Craig, was convinced as well, and the pair of them immediately started choosing their lots. Sewall selected frontage on the north side of the river right near the falls and began felling trees. Craig found a shallow vale to his liking not far from a tributary called Dyer Brook. Soon after, the group departed, returning to the coast.

That fall, Levi came back with his oldest son, David, then seventeen. In the intervening months, Levi had arranged to buy the one-mile-square plot at the site, including the falls, from the Commonwealth of Massachusetts, which held the deed. He had acted also on behalf of Jesse Craig, including Craig's five acres as well.

Father and son began to construct a house at the site, "shingling" the roof of the rough structure with spruce bark. Three thousand square feet of boards for the roof, floors, and walls were brought in by raft, along with a cookstove and various provisions. The stove and supplies were offloaded about a half mile above the falls, but Levi thought that they could move the lumber closer by using a snubline gripped by men on either side of the stream. Too late he learned just how strong the Mattawamkeag was—the wood got away from them and tumbled over the falls. David had the unenviable task of salvaging what he could and hauling it back up to the home site.

Soon winter was closing in, and when the temperatures turned too cold to work any longer, they broke for home. They were back like flowers in the spring, however, this time accompanied by another son, Sam. The threesome stayed with a family friend in the nearby hamlet of Crystal. For weeks they made the six-mile trek from there to their clearing, spending long days sawing and hammering.

Slowly the house began to take shape. It was sixteen feet wide and twenty-six feet long, made of squared logs and shingled, with floors of wide pine boards scrubbed until they were white. A simple Cape, it had a kitchen and two bedrooms downstairs and one large room upstairs with windows at either end.

By July of 1843, it was ready for the family to move. Levi and his second son, Sam, loaded Rebecca and the small boys, George and Otis, into a canoe and paddled it down Fish Stream into the Mattawamkeag River. Daughters Sarah and Pauline walked through the woods from Patten via Crystal on the trail their father and brothers had trod on their trips back and forth.

Between the house and the barn the men built another outbuilding. Soon pink and white roses would decorate the front yard and hops and grapevines would grow near the entryway. They planted apple trees and lilacs, and Sarah kept flower gardens. Down over the bank in front of the house the river rushed by.

That first summer Jesse Craig lived with the Sewalls, felling trees to build his own home. While he worked, the family cleared more land and planted potatoes, corn, and beans between the stumps. For other provisions they made trips to Patten, eleven miles distant, or to Crystal over a rough tote road. When the water level was high enough, they traveled by canoe, but at other times Levi and the boys carried in the supplies themselves. Bill Sewall remembered his father telling him that he once humped ninety pounds of flour six miles on his back.

Levi and Rebecca spent their first years in Island Falls simply getting acclimated to life in the woods. "The family were now settled in the midst of a vast forest with no road on the west nearer than Crystal Mill and none on the east nearer than Smyrna Mills on the East Branch,"[10] as a history of The County puts it. Which is to say there wasn't another settlement, nor even a road, for five miles in one direction and ten in the other. Neither of the Sewalls had any previous experience in primitive living. But, as Bill said later, "I think they were calculated for pioneer people. They liked the life and had no fear of anything in the woods."[11]

Indeed, it would be hard to find a couple more suited to it. Being a cobbler and something of a mechanic from his days in the machine shop, Levi Sewall could make or fix just about anything, from shoes to furniture. Skilled with a needle, Rebecca was able to sew the family all the clothes they needed for each season. The couple sold the three horses they had brought with them from Phippsburg and bought cows they could graze on the surrounding grass. Later Levi would also acquire a team of oxen, and he began to work the woods with his older sons. They'd fell trees, drag them to the river, and sell them to the drivers who shepherded the timber down the river toward Bangor. Working ceaselessly, Sewall was able to ease the circumstances of the family little by little. Under his tutelage—and that of a Penobscot Indian neighbor—David and Sam Sewall became fairly expert woodsmen.

Within a year other families were moving into the settlement. The Craigs had finished their home and moved in. The Youngs and Hansons built houses alongside the river or on the approaches into town. The Lurveys arrived and so did the Hardings. Island Falls was growing.

Rebecca Sewall was also growing, and on April 13, 1845, she and Levi welcomed their newest arrival, William Wingate, the first white child born in Island Falls. They named the boy after a logger who camped not far from their home on the Mattawamkeag. When he heard that Rebecca was pregnant, he'd asked the couple to name the baby after him. A strong, stalwart, honest man, Wingate had many qualities the couple hoped their child would exhibit one day, and they agreed.

Bill was their sixth child behind Dave, Sam, Sarah, Pauline, and George (Otis having died as a toddler before Bill was born). William Wingate Sewall almost met the same fate. He was a weak newborn, so near death at birth that his mother couldn't tell whether he was breathing. The boy's early years were plagued by a succession of colds and flu—potentially life-threatening illnesses on the Maine frontier—and his colds often led to dangerous ear infections. Rebecca didn't dare wean Bill until he was approaching three, and his early years were spent in bed, slathered in mustard plasters, being read to by his sisters. Up to the age of six, Sewall was infirm in one way or another half the time, and for years after that he continued to have problems with his ears, which bothered him when he got them wet or when it was deeply cold.

Though there was no formal school in Island Falls until Bill was almost too old to attend, he was a bright child and managed to learn quite a bit on his own. His eldest sister Sarah taught "school" at the Jesse Craig house as early as 1847 for the children of the two families, and it was she who gave Bill the gift of reading. His brother Sam showed him how to write his name.

The academy of nature proved to be his favorite classroom, though, and he learned much simply by following his father and older brothers around. Little Bill's first gun came when he was seven, about the time he was allowed to handle a canoe by himself, and he loved the confidence and freedom these two tools afforded him.

Almost immediately he began hunting, his first kill a squirrel. At the time he was still so small that he could barely heft the gun to make the shot, and he certainly couldn't hold it steady, so one of his brothers bent down so Bill could rest the gun barrel on his back. The boy's aim proved true, the quarry fell from the tree, and the excited little hunter scurried over to pick up his prize. The dazed rodent promptly bit him—hard enough that he had to pry its jaws from his hand. Hunting lesson number one. Before long, though, the boy was shooting partridges, then deer. By the time he was twelve he was guiding other hunters.[12]

His tutors, older brothers Dave and Sam, were patient with him. Like their father—and so many other pioneers—they had learned by doing. The first winter the family spent in their new home, a Native American named Tomah set up camp within a few hundred feet of their door. He soon made an arrangement with the newcomers—he would provide them with meat in exchange for flour and vegetables. This was a better deal than it looked, because both Sewall boys tagged along with Tomah when he went hunting and fishing, and they studied everything he did. Young, smart, and eager, they picked up skills quickly. Tomah would call the moose in, and Dave, who had a steady hand, a fine gun, and a good eye, would do the shooting.

Dave was a capable young man and a particular inspiration to young Bill. Not only had he become skilled as a builder, hunter, and fisherman, but he had an engaging confidence, a sureness about him. When he was still a scrawny sixteen-year-old, all of 110 pounds, he had faced down a drunk hunter who threatened to knife him. Dave had simply picked up his fowling gun and told the man to sit down and sleep it off—which he did. Later, Dave saw to it that the hungover Nimrod was fed and then escorted him back to Crystal.

By the time little Bill was born, both Dave and Sam were employed in the woods, cutting wood in the winter and driving logs in the spring. They had attended school through their mid-teens back in Phippsburg, but began to do adult work as soon as they moved to The County. They proved to be as suited to river driving as they were to hunting and fishing. Dave became widely known for his expertise with an ax after rescuing a pair of oxen while working as a teamster. The team was hauling a sled laden with logs down a steep incline, and the load was so heavy that the sled picked up speed and dragged the two oxen off the road. They hit a tree, which snapped in two and caught on the yoke joining the two animals, lifting them right off the ground by their necks. The only way to save the big beasts was to split the yoke with an ax—instantly, before the animals strangled. Everything about the strike had to be exact—too far to either side and he'd kill an ox. In a split second Dave made the cut cleanly.

Sam was just as able. For a couple of winters, he was employed by a party of surveyors who were working up on the Fish and Aroostook rivers, spending months in the woods with them. He came back "an expert woodsman," according to Bill.[13] And he brought a gift for his little brother—a compass. The small instrument gave the boy even more self-confidence than the canoe and the gun had earlier. "I very soon got so I had no fear of getting lost," he'd remember later.[14] Nor was he particularly afraid of any of the critters he encountered, be they bear, moose, or wolf.

Levi had taught him a lesson that he always remembered and later passed on to the clients of his guide service: "[D]on't get scared of anything until it hurts you, and you won't get scared very often."[15] With his rifle, his boat, and his compass he felt he could go anywhere. "It was then my chief delight to get off into the woods out of sight of an opening," he wrote.[16]

While the boy flourished in the woods on his own, his parents nonetheless thought it important that he receive some formal schooling. At age eleven Bill was shuttled off to New Limerick, twenty miles away, to stay with his sister Pauline, now married and settled there with her husband, Oliver Dow. Slightly larger than Island Falls, New Limerick had a small school.

Pauline had a little boy, Wilmot, just old enough to toddle around, and when he wasn't in class, Bill set about schooling the young fellow in the outdoors, just as his brothers had him. It was the beginning of the lifelong bond between the two.

Bill stayed with Pauline until he took sick once again, and when he finally regained his health back home in Island Falls, he traveled to school in Patten to study in the eight- to twelve-week sessions offered there. The rest of his time was spent helping his father with farm chores and hunting and exploring during those glorious free hours.

In 1859, when Bill was fourteen, the residents of Island Falls decided it was time the community had its own school. The teenager was part of the crew that built the rough log cabin, then he put away his hammer to attend classes in the new school's inaugural year. There were about twenty other students, some of whom traveled great distances to be there, usually in the deep of winter. Sessions would run for three months in the winter, and also for a short period in summer. Already accomplished as an outdoorsman, Sewall found himself just as drawn to books—particularly poetry and adventure stories.

The year 1861 was a historic one both for the nation and for Bill Sewall. When armies of men from the North rushed southward to try and preserve the Union, Bill's older brother George and a few dozen other men from Island Falls were among them. ("At the outbreak of the Civil War," Sewall recalled, "there were forty-two voters in the plantation of Island Falls. During the war there were forty-four men who went into the Union army from our settlement.")[17]

Bill was off to a life-changing experience of his own—his first log drive. The crew he was hired on to was among the last to move timber for a while. Due to shortages caused by the war, times were becoming increasingly rough. "I got only half my pay," he wrote later, and "all business came to a standstill; there was no sale for logs after they were taken to the booms at Old Town."[18]

Epic change had recently come to the woods of Maine, too. Several years prior, lumbermen had begun commercial harvesting of spruce, and they started in the Mattawamkeag area. "[It] was the first winter that many spruce logs were cut in our vicinity," Sewall remembered later. "That was the beginning of the destruction of the spruce trees in northern Maine."[19]

Until the 1850s, the primary target for lumbermen had been eastern white pine, and Bangor, ninety miles south of Island Falls, had ridden the sappy timber to fame and fortune. The tall pines had been valuable commodities ever since 1605, when explorer George Weymouth brought some pine masts back to England. Lightweight and easy to work, the wood quickly became sought after for shipbuilding and house construction. By the 1830s Bangor (known as the Queen City) was the largest lumber port in the world and one of the most important cities in the nation. But pine wood became so valuable that the species was almost cut out of existence, and commercial timber operators began looking for alternatives. There were millions of acres of pine's coniferous cousin, the spruce, in the North Woods, and some loggers had been talking about its potential uses since the 1840s, but were considered "mad or, at best, addlepated"[20] for considering the market value of a "weed tree."

In the spring of 1861, Sewall walked into Patten to get his first set of caulks made. These were the spiked boots that helped drivers stay upright on floating lengths of timber. The blacksmith crafted some spikes, his brother fixed them to his boots, and he was ready.

The lumber camp he reported to was on Dyer Brook, the small tributary of the Mattawamkeag River on the north side of town, and the walk in was about nine miles. The snows were deep the morning Sewall headed off, but he reached camp by lunchtime and worked the afternoon. Within a few hours he had already gone into the frigid water twice—not uncommon for a tenderfoot—and that first night he slept in his wet clothes.

Timber was cut in the winter when the ground was frozen, making it easier to drag with oxen. Loads were hauled to great piles by the river's edge, and when the spring thaw came, tier after tier of timbers were tumbled into the swollen river to be floated down to Mattawamkeag Lake. There they'd be collected behind a boom—made by connecting the longest spruce logs—and rafted across the big basin as a single unit.

River driving posed innumerable dangers. The water could be too high or too low. "Breaking the landing," the process of pushing the first logs into the stream and setting up the rest to follow, was particularly precarious: the staggering weight of the timber could cause the piles to collapse unexpectedly and pin or trap a man. When the trees started to go, drivers would often have to jump into the water and swim for the opposite shore with the whole mass of logs tumbling behind them, and over the years many men ended up trapped underneath them. The logs could get tangled into jams, which often occurred when one log got perpendicular to the others at a point where the watercourse narrowed. It would fetch up, and soon a wall of timbers, sometimes fifteen or twenty feet high, would develop as each successive log slammed into the others. This, in turn, would dam up the water behind the jam, compounding the problem. The weight of wood and water would cause an enormous tension that was always a hazard to deal with. To break the jam, men would have to get at the "key" log, and the only way to do that was to cut and move several other logs while tons of force pressed against the very trees they were astride.

Bill Sewall encountered many of these challenges his first year. There were simple adventures—walking four miles to carry forty-pound bags of flour and salt pork back to camp—and situations with much more menacing potential— falling into the river with the logs queuing up behind him and finding no place to climb out due to dense alder brush along the riverbanks. Rewards for his labor, he reported, included the worst camp food he'd ever eat in a forty-year career and half the pay he had expected.

The next year, though, he was back.

When summer came in 1861, Bill and Sam took a job cutting wood on four acres about nine miles from their home. Each day, they'd load up provisions, hike in, and work as long as there was enough light. This earned them twelve dollars in four days. Bill donated his share to an Island Falls man who had a family to support and no income. "That was the way the old-time people dealt with their neighbors up here in the woods,"[21] he later explained.

When the Sewall brothers came back into town from a stint in the woods, they'd seek out news of the war. Talk was all over town of soldiers killed in action. In 1862 the village began a battle of its own.

"The children were nearly all dying of diptheria," Sewall would later recount. "I knew families of five children where every one of them died, and hardly a family escaped without losing some children." The teenager watched as a neighbor built a small coffin each day for five days straight to be delivered to a family in Crystal. The epidemic had begun in military camps and was spread to the woodland settlements by returning soldiers. The Sewalls were not spared; the plague claimed Bill's brother George. "My first great sorrow and a great grief," he termed it, "for George was a favorite with all,"[22] Less than eight months later, younger brother Fred was gone, too.

Dave Sewall would contract the disease and survive but lose a baby to it. Two of Sam's children died, and his wife lost her sister. Bill himself fell victim and was desperately ill for almost a month, his heart stopping on three different occasions. His parents assumed they would lose him, too, and the doctor gave him only a slight chance of making it.

The young man had a tenacious spirit, though, and fought his way back to health. He suffered the aftereffects for months to come. His hands and feet would occasionally go numb, as if they were asleep, causing him to collapse. For extended periods he also lost his voice and his eyesight.

The diphtheria epidemic ravaged Island Falls for about a year, and the entire community took a long time to recover. But spring came again and when it did, Bill was back on the log drive. Like so many Mainers then—and even now—life was a seasonal cycle, and every couple of months brought a new occupation. In summer, the young man worked for his father on the farm. Autumn he spent hunting and trapping. Furs were fetching high prices, and Bill and Sam collected their share. Winters, Sewall and his brothers returned to the lumber camps.

When he was in camp, Bill Sewall was more than a casual apprentice. Just as his brothers had watched the Native Tomah closely, Bill carefully observed each aspect of river driving. While the boys of his age took off to drink away their woods wages, he filled diaries. "I was anxious to learn all the arts of the lumber business,"[23] he said later. And learn he did.

This was typical of Sewall. If he had an interest, he followed it almost obsessively. When he was a young man, he met a native couple who had come to camp by the Mattawamkeag and gather basketmaking supplies. Sewall marched over to visit on a few occasions, both to be neighborly and because he wanted an authentic birchbark canoe. The man agreed to make him one. Rather than go off and wait patiently for the boat to be delivered, though, Sewall was eager to observe and help with every phase, from gathering "winter birch," the tougher, hardier skin of large birch trees, to constructing the cedar frame. He was bitterly frustrated when other work kept taking him away from the project.

By 1865—when he was only twenty—Sewall put the knowledge he'd been accumulating to work and assembled his own logging crew. Young and gung-ho—most of the members of his crew were older than he was—he was determined to run the kind of operation he would want to work for himself. "I did not ask any man to do anything I could not do or to do more than I could do,"[24] he'd explain later. Fair treatment, honest work, good food, and a hot fire to warm them and dry their clothes, these he considered rights not privileges.

It wasn't long before loggers throughout the North Woods were talking about Bill Sewall and his crew. In May of 1866, he pulled a stunt that brought him even wider notice. The dam at Chamberlain Lake, which controlled the water flow on the Allagash River, had been a source of much contention ever since its construction in 1841. Tolls for moving logs through were considered high, and thugs were often hired to guard the great bulwark, because mill owners would blow it up again and again. The caretakers would frequently hold the water back to favor whichever driver they wanted to help. When that happened, crews downstream wouldn't have enough flow to move their logs, and they'd have to portage at particularly dry spots. That was the case during this particular spring drive. Crews had spent a week portaging at the dry flats near Edmundston.[25]

This extra work didn't sit well with Sewall. When his team's efforts were stalled due to the closed dam, he and six of his men rowed to the famous dam in a bateau, hauled up the gates, and spiked them open, washing his timber down to Grand Falls. The drivers downstream watched as the river all of sudden began to rise and Sewall and his men roared past with their logs, hooting and hollering.[26]

This was the sort of gutsiness that made a river driver's name.

By the late 1860s, Levi and Rebecca Sewall were beginning to slow down, and Bill thought it was time they had a more comfortable home. Their original cabin was small, dark, and rough, and the village was growing all around it. Bill and his father consulted with a local builder, Osgood Pingree, to help them plan and build a new place, and Sewall agreed to work with him when he wasn't working in the woods, mostly in the heat of summer.

The new structure would be just up the road from the original and much closer to the center of Island Falls. It would be three stories and about five times larger than their previous home. With its austere white facade, twin chimneys, and porch, it would be one of the few houses in town built from lumber rather than squared logs, and one of the finest Island Falls had ever seen. The building project took years, and in December of 1870 the family finally moved in. Not only was the new Sewall house a showplace, but it would become perhaps the most important house in the burgeoning town.

In 1856 the land in the village had been measured and lotted by a surveyor from Haynesville, and the plots—a quarter-mile square, or 160 acres—had been offered for sale to settlers. Soon they came. In a few years the population rose to 132, with 25 families. The Aroostook hamlet was achieving critical mass, and in order to receive state funds for schooling and to collect taxes, it had to get organized. In 1858 the little settlement founded by Levi Sewall officially became Island Falls Plantation.

The Sewalls continued to play central roles in the new town—Levi Sewall would be the first moderator of business, his son Dave the first assessor. Funds were dutifully raised to build a schoolhouse—Levi Sewall, superintendent—and by the time the Sewall house was finished, there were twenty-two kids attending class.[27] In 1863, Levi Sewall became the first postmaster for Island Falls and his house served as the post office. This put the Sewalls right at the heart of the community—and at this moment in history, it was really beginning to beat.

In the 1860 census every man in town was listed as a farmer, but most worked in the woods and ran other concerns as well. In 1862 Dave brought industry to town by building the first sawmill. He made lumber and shingles until 1889, when he sold the business. Bill's own enterprise was coming along nicely, too. With a fine new family home and a successful logging company—and status as the town's most eligible bachelor—Bill Sewall had most of what he could have wanted.

But he had friends who had gone to Minnesota to find their fortune in the lumber business, and he had an itch to join them. Logging was further behind in that territory than in Maine—Minnesota wouldn't reach its lumbering peak until 1930—and a lot of Mainers were heading west to help get it going. Sewall's buddies wrote letters regaling him with the remunerative details—a hundred dollars a month for a man who was as skilled as he—and the venturesome young woodsman was much intrigued. But his parents were in frail health and he didn't dare leave them. "I may have lost a great financial opportunity," he would later write, "but I had the satisfaction of doing my duty. I have tried to put duty foremost throughout my life."[28] The temptation was there. Many of the Island Falls men who had left to fight in the Civil War had found new homes in other parts of the country. This was the first hint that Sewall would consider doing so himself.

A Grander, More Beautiful Sight

Roosevelt would return to Island Falls at the end of February 1879, just six months after his first visit. It had been a little over a year since his father passed away, and his grief had abated. School was going better—his social world was expanding, he'd joined fraternal organizations, he had his routines down. And he'd made a new acquaintance who would have a large impact on his well being—Alice Hathaway Lee. TR had been spending a great deal of time with the Lee family in Chestnut Hill, just outside Boston, driving over from Cambridge with his one-horse "dogcart" to see her whenever he could. This didn't deter him from paying attention to the other young ladies he encountered, however—"Met a pretty Miss Cross,"[1] he wrote in his diary just a day after a sledding trip at Alice Lee's—but none seemed to captivate him the way this beauty did.

His father was still never far from his thoughts. TR marked the anniversary of his passing by writing a letter home and by fretting about whether he could be the kind of son his father would have admired. "O' God give me strength to live as he would have wished me!"[2] he wrote in his diary. Just before departing for Island Falls he had attended a dinner at the Porcellian Club, a prestigious social club at Harvard, where he had met older men who had known his father personally or by reputation, and while he was pleased that many had fond remembrances of Theodore Roosevelt, Sr., he continued to doubt that he could live up to the family name.

All that was put to the back of Roosevelt's mind as he boarded the 7 p.m. train for Mattawamkeag on February 27. He'd arranged to spend a couple of weeks with Bill Sewall by himself this time. The train sped through the night and reached the Aroostook County outpost at 11:00 the next morning. Sewall was waiting for him with a sleigh.

The trip to Island Falls again took all day. The air was frigid, but they were well prepared, and TR was so happy to be back that he enjoyed the ride despite the fact that for much of the way they were breaking trail. The snow was about three feet deep in most places, drifting to six, and the road in those days often saw so little traffic in winter that drivers essentially had to plow it themselves, which made for a slow and bumpy ride.[3]

Client and guide were off to the woods the next day, inviting Will Dow along and putting in six miles over deep snow on snowshoes. TR had never used the big ash-and-lash footgear before. They were usually awkward and cumbersome for novices, but he found he "got along very well"[4] as they made the rounds of Will Dow's "lucivee" traps. This was a name used for the Canada lynx, an animal that haunted the northern Maine woods but was rarely seen. The elusive cat had an array of names—*loup cervier*, Indian devil, wildcat, bob-cat, catamount, and "wolverene"—and because of its secretive nature, legends abounded about it, usually involving the grisly dismemberment of loggers.

They found sign from lucivees (lynx), foxes, otters, and rabbits, but Dow's traps were empty. TR spotted a porcupine way up in a hemlock tree, and the prickly animal didn't last long on his perch. "I brought him down quite neatly with the rifle," TR wrote in his diary.[5] Why he felt the need to drop a porky is another question.

The budding conservationist in him was quite smitten with the surroundings, perhaps even more so than on his visit in September. "The woods looked simply perfect,"[6] he wrote in his diary. "I can not get used to the extreme beauty of the snow-covered pine and spruce forests." He penned his mother a glowing letter that used almost the exact same language: "I have never seen a grander or more beautiful sight than the northern woods in winter. The evergreens laden with snow make the most beautiful contrast of green and white, and when it freezes after a rain all the trees look as though they were made of crystal. The snow under foot being about three feet deep, and drifting to twice that depth in places, completely changes the aspect of things."[7]

On Sunday he read his Bible, as was his custom, though he didn't allow himself to be housebound by his habit. He trudged out to a point near the south end of Mattawamkeag Lake, near the confluence of the West Branch of the Mattawamkeag River and First Brook, where the huge water body narrows back into a river. Roosevelt found this lakeside grove, sloping down to the water, especially picturesque and peaceful, and he returned there so many times during his stays in Island Falls that it now has been designated a Maine Historic Site called Bible Point.

Will Dow caught up with Roosevelt the next day and took him up Dyer Brook, the stream that tumbles through Island Falls from the north, feeding into the river. The pair trekked along it for a couple of miles and then ventured into the deeper forest, which was utterly tranquil. The hunter in TR wanted more game than he was finding—"there is very little life in the woods"—he wrote in his diary.[8] Ever the curious naturalist, however, he still managed to spot Arctic woodpeckers, chickadees, and whiskeyjacks, the colorful Canada or gray jays. Looking like giant chickadees, with the gregarious personalities to match, gray jays were so common at encampments in the Maine woods that they inspired a wealth of nicknames—gorbies, meat birds, moose birds, venison hawks, camp robbers. Roosevelt and Dow also saw hare and lynx prints, and the spot where a spruce partridge had passed the night. "But in an eight-hour tramp, these were the only traces of life," TR lamented.[9] The winter woods were made for stealth.

Out again with Bill Sewall the next day, sloshing through wet snow on a warm afternoon, he found the situation much the same. The pair discovered many tracks—fox, rabbit, otter, mink, weasel, squirrel, porcupine—but the only breathing animals were the two of them and the chickadees and woodpeckers they'd seen before. A set of partridge prints did lead the young hunter to a genuine grouse, though, and he brought it home for supper.

No matter where they tramped in the Mattawamkeag region, Roosevelt's luck continued this way, though he and his guide did manage to trap a lynx and a fox. That the young hunter was having a good time despite finding nothing to draw down upon, is testament to both his appreciation for these woodlands and his deepening friendship with his guides. For many outdoorsmen of his day, the fun of hunting was all in the shooting, but not for TR. "Spent the day snowshoeing through the woods as usual—and with my usual ill success as regards game," he wrote. "Otherwise I am enjoying myself to the utmost, but the asthma keeps me up a good deal at night."[10] Sewall and the Maine woods were working their magic on the young city dweller.

With little luck finding furbearers to fire at, Sewall and Dow introduced TR to another denizen of the Maine woods—the lumberman. On a Wednesday in March, they sat down to lunch at a nearby logging camp. The following day the trio hitched a pung—a small, boxy sleigh—to a scruffy-looking horse and set off for a camp thirty miles distant in the Oxbow region, a densely wooded area where the Aroostook River almost makes a perfect circle.

To reach that territory—more remote even than Island Falls, which was among the wildest places TR had ever been in his young life—they traveled north over several rugged woods roads. By the time they arrived at another set of logging camps it was well after dark and the temperature was ten below.

Roosevelt, Sewall, and Dow spent a few days in camp, a logging operation no doubt run by a friend of Sewall's. They were allowed to eat and bunk with the crew, and when the loggers left for a long day of cutting, TR and his guides set out after game.

Maine lumber camps during this era were primitive, hard, and dirty places. The structures were typically built of rough, notched logs, constructed using no nails and only axes for tools, shingled with cedar shakes and chinked with moss and mud. Floors were usually earth but sometimes covered with pine boughs. Single cookstoves or barrel woodstoves provided heat, and men slept either side by side under the same covers on one large bed or in individual bunks. Absent were any creature comforts—men worked and slept in the same clothes day after day, and often didn't even remove their boots before they went to bed for fear they wouldn't be able to pull them back on over their swollen, wet feet the next morning. Lice were common, and to be rid of them clothes were sometimes boiled, other times sprinkled with salt. The workday started at 4 a.m. and lasted until 9 p.m. with four meals of salt cod, beanhole beans, sourdough biscuits, and pickled beef, sometimes followed by a song, a tall tale, or a game of cards. Drinking and fights were not rare. In all ways it was an intense experience—the work was dangerous and difficult, the crowding constant, the living primal—yet many lumbermen swore they wouldn't trade it for anything.

The day after their arrival, Dow and TR left early in the morning, trekking through a heavy snow, on their first hunting trip in the Oxbow. They passed the morning scouting—again, for anything—and this time hit it big.

"[We] roused a caribou in a dense, low spruce wood," Roosevelt recorded in his diary.[11] They followed the beast far into the thick woodlands, but could never catch up with it. Rather than bivouac in the wild with little food and no blankets, they finally abandoned their chase and returned to camp.

Early the next morning, though, the two were out again, eager to pick up the track of the caribou. The morning air was bitingly cold, well below zero. Dow was able to find the animal's prints, and they crept along the trail even though it dragged them through cedar swamps, over hardwood ridges, through hemlock woods, and across cranberry bogs. When walking or running became too hard in the three-foot-deep snow, the caribou would bound ahead—an option not available to Roosevelt and Dow. For them it was simply a difficult slog. After spending most of the day in chase without even a glimpse of their quarry, they returned to camp by sunset.

By day three, after wading through miles of deep and wet snow, TR elected to rest in camp. This allowed the snowshoeing to improve—with a little help from some freezing rain that put a crust over the snow—and it gave Roosevelt some time among the men, great fun as it turned out. "I like these lumbermen very much, and get on capitally with them—great rough, hospitable fellows," he wrote in his diary. "I am great friends with one especial, Charley Brown." Roosevelt became chummy enough with the Civil War vet to stop by and see him at his house later, and he was "as much struck with his good and pretty wife as I had been with him."[12]

Sewall was quite impressed how well the slight, brainy, city boy related to these unsophisticated woodsmen. "The reason that he knew so much about everything, I found, was that wherever he went he got in with the right people,"[13] Sewall would later report. "Old woodsmen, they were, who did not know anything but the woods. I doubt if they could have written their names, but they knew the woods, the whole of them, and they knew all of the hardships connected with pioneer life. They had gone in up to Ox Bow on the Aroostook River, and it was a long ways from the road. The river was their road, and they had managed to live there, mostly by hunting. Theodore enjoyed them immensely."[14]

They no doubt appreciated him, too, if for nothing else than the spread that he laid out for them on his last night in camp. While out snowshoeing that day, Roosevelt and Sewall had happened upon a deer yard, and the boy picked out a good-looking deer and fired a shot at its head but missed. The animal bolted, and TR took off in hot pursuit, running after it "at full speed about a mile,"[15] before getting another shot. This time he hit his target. He and Sewall hauled the meat back to camp, where it was prepared for "a royal venison supper," as Roosevelt put it. "A pleasant change from the ordinary routine of pork and beans."[16] This was TR's first deer, and he was so pleased that he gifted Sewall with a Winchester rifle, a prize that Sewall passed down to his son.[17]

The dinner marked the high point of their lumber camp sojourn, and the trio turned back toward Island Falls in the morning. Sewall remembered Roosevelt's reaction to the loggers: "He told me after he left the camp how glad he was that he had met them. He said that he could read about such things, but here he had first-hand accounts of backwoods life from the men who had lived it and knew what they were talking about. Even then he was quick to find the real man in very simple men."[18]

Back in Island Falls, Roosevelt wrote his mother: "I visited two lumber camps, staying at one four days. It was great fun to see such a perfectly unique type of life."[19] Somehow the frozen air and hard living agreed with the young man. In his letter he attributed his improving health to the woods life. "The first two or three days I had asthma," he wrote, "but, funnily enough, this left me entirely as soon as I went into camp."[20] Even the frigid temperatures were no problem. "The thermometer was below zero pretty often, but I was not bothered by the cold at all. . . . in the woods the wind never blows, and as long as we were moving about it made little difference how low the temperature was, but sitting still for lunch we felt it immediately."[21]

The three companions would feel it again on the trek back to Island Falls. It wasn't that the thermometer was falling but that the rain and sleet were, making the snow too mushy for the pung. Their horse lost the track several times, foundering in deep snow. Over and over they had to hop down, unharness the animal, drag the pung back onto the road, and hitch up the horse again. "It was very fatiguing work, as we walked all the time, and got wet through, cold, and hungry," Roosevelt noted in his diary.[22] Some snow buntings sang to cheer them as they went, though, and they made Island Falls in late afternoon, just in time for tea. The warmth and soft comforts of the Sewall House must have been a relief.

If Roosevelt was tired from the hardships he'd been facing over the past few days, he didn't show it. He had Sewall and Dow back out in the wild the following morning, checking the lynx traps. The young hunter bagged a raccoon and two grouse as they walked, but once again they found their snares empty. That night they built a shelter on the shore of Mattawmakeag Lake and made camp. Roosevelt would always remember these "delicious nights. . . on balsam boughs in front of a blazing stump, when we had beaten down and shoveled away the deep snow."[23]

In returning home to Island Falls on Thursday, they walked the whole way on the frozen lake and river, only using their snowshoes about half the time. No game revealed itself, so they played a game of their own by taking very long-range shots with their rifles. "All three of us made very good shots with the 'old reliable' (Sharp's business no. 45)"Roosevelt recorded in his diary.[24]

Again on Friday they walked the trap line and hunted partridges, but again they were unsuccessful.

While TR would no doubt have preferred more action, he enjoyed himself immensely. As his second trip to Island Falls came to a close, he gushed in his journal: "I have had a good success with this trip," and "I have never passed a pleasanter two weeks. The skins of the fox, lucivee, coon, and buck made quite a set of trophies; and we have shot enough partridges and rabbits to eat—not to mention the venison. I have collected a good many specimens."[25] His plan was to have the fox and the lynx skins made into rugs for Alice and another of his lady friends.

Just a week back from Island Falls, TR boxed for the lightweight division cup at Harvard. He defeated his first opponent but eventually lost to the champion, a boy named Hanks. One has to wonder how his travels in the Maine woods prepared him for his bouts. Some inkling was contained in a note he dashed off to his mother: "[I] feel that I have got enough health to last me till next summer."[26]

Tough as a Pine Knot

T he Maine woods beckoned once more the following August, and again, Roosevelt had much on his mind. This time it wasn't family issues but rather the question that faces everyone coming to the end of their schooling—what next? Of course, he had some ideas, which he recorded in his diary: "I am thinking pretty seriously as to what I shall do when I leave College; I shall probably either pursue a scientific course, or else study law, preparatory to going into public life."[1]

He was also thinking pretty seriously about his friend Alice Lee, so much that it seems he was debating whether or not he wanted to travel north again to join his cousin and others at Bill Sewall's. "Went in town to see the girls—Rose, Rosy, and Alice—off to the Slades," he noted. "They wanted me very much to go down to stay a few days with them; and they were all so cordial, and Alice was so bewitchingly pretty that it was frightfully hard to refuse; I took the night train for Mattawamkeag, however, as I agreed to meet Emlen."[2]

This time it was Dave Sewall, Bill's older brother, who met TR at Mattawamkeag Station at 10 a.m. Dave was almost as colorful a character as his brother, and Roosevelt would tell several stories about him for years to come.

Decades later, for instance, TR would summon up Dave's droll way with words to help extricate himself from a political jam. After TR's unsuccessful second run for the presidency on the Bull Moose ticket in 1912, Roosevelt used the expression "weasel words" to describe something said by winning candidate Woodrow Wilson. The term was quickly added to the long Roosevelt lexicon and had begun seeping into popular culture, when someone pointed out that it had been used years before in *Century Magazine* and accusations of plagiarism were raised.

Ever the writer and ever the fighter, Roosevelt wanted to clear his name, and he told a *New York Times* reporter how he happened to come up with the expression. "About thirty-seven years ago," he explained, "I was going up a mountain in the Maine woods in a carriage, driven by Bill Sewall's brother, Dave Sewall. We saw an old man along the roadside with whom Dave was acquainted. When we had passed, Dave Sewall said: 'That there man can do a lot of funny things with this language of ours. He can take a word and weasel it around and suck the meat out of it like a weasel sucks the meat out of an egg, until it don't mean anything at all, no matter what it sounds like it means.'"³

That episode might well have taken place during this summer trip to Island Falls. It might also have been during this trip that Roosevelt asked Dave Sewall—as they navigated a particularly wet and rocky backwoods byway—how people in Aroostook County told the difference between roads and rivers. "No beaver dams in the roads,"⁴ quipped Sewall. Whatever they were discussing, the pair drove up to meet Emlen Roosevelt and Arthur Cutler, who awaited them at the Sewall House.

This late summer trip had a special allure for Roosevelt. The plan was to climb Katahdin, something he'd wanted to do since he first saw Maine's highest peak from the window of the Sewall House. As a well-read natural-history lover, Roosevelt was surely aware of Henry David Thoreau's *The Maine Woods*, published fifteen years earlier, and perhaps also of writings by Harvard geology professor Charles E. Hamlin, who had studied the mountain, beginning in the 1860s. By the time Roosevelt would tackle it, Katahdin was renowned.

Bill Sewall himself had been up the mountain a few times already; the first was in September of 1867, when he was about the age Roosevelt was on this trip. He had climbed in a party that included his sister Sarah and brother Sam, Sam's wife, Nancy, and one other—"I decided to let my nephew Wilmot Dow, who was then a boy of twelve years, go with us also."⁵ The expedition lasted a week, with plenty of fishing, hunting, and berrying along the way, and Sewall was convinced that their climb had historic significance. "So far as we were able to learn," he offered, "only two women had ever climbed the mountain previous[ly]."⁶

During his first day back in Island Falls in August 1879, Theodore Roosevelt spent most of his time visiting with everyone in the household and preparing a pack for the ascent. The load he put together was more than adequate, including everything from toiletries to weaponry: "I have two complete changes of clothes, and plenty of handkerchiefs and woolen socks. I dress in a flannel shirt, light, strong duck trousers and heavy underflannels; carry heavy jacket and a blanket—and have my necessaries in a small bag. I have taken both rifle and shotgun."⁷ All told, his haversack weighed forty-five pounds, including his guns and ammunition, which is not bad for a trip of several days. Rather than haul all their food, the party would hunt and fish along the way.⁸

The following morning, he and Emlen struck out for their old camp at Mattawamkeag Lake without a guide to accompany them. They were familiar with the terrain by now, and they paddled down to the foot of the lake and hunted for partridges for part of the day, finding none. They did, however, "pick up a duck in the thoroughfare."[9] TR seemed to enjoy the company of his fellow New Yorkers almost as much as he did Sewall and Dow. "Em and Arthur are capital fellows for a trip of this kind—unselfish, good natured, and not minding a little fatigue and hardship," he wrote.[10]

The five of them—TR, Emlen, Cutler, Sewall, and Dow—started out for Katahdin on August 26. From Island Falls to Katahdin Lake it's about thirty-five miles, and the party drove by buckboard for the first twenty-three and then humped their packs for the next ten. At Wassataquoik Stream, a roiling, rock-studded tributary of the East Branch of the Penobscot, TR suffered a setback while trying to make it across barefoot. He dropped one of the shoes he was carrying and the current took it before he could grab hold of it. As a result, when he reached shore he had to switch to the only alternative footgear he had—the soft-soled moccasins he had brought along to use as slippers.[11]

The next day he put on his moccasins and padded his way up to the head of Katahdin Lake where they set up camp within sight of the towering peak. The seven-hundred-acre lake is flush with trout, and the Great Basin of Katahdin looks so lofty four miles away that it all but casts a shadow. Roosevelt and Sewall and their friends likely camped at the north end of the lake, enjoying the spectacular view. Here TR bagged four ducks, two grouse, and a couple of trout to add to their daily take. After supper, they sat around and chatted. "It is very pleasant and like old times in the evenings," Roosevelt wrote, "round the roaring logs of the campfire."[12]

The next day they started toward the base of the mountain after lunch. TR had already put in five miles tramping around in the woods in search of partridges. They caught "about 100 trout at Sandy Brook," before getting lost in a thicket. Once free of the tangle, they set up camp near a watering hole, "wet, tired, and hungry—but happy."[13] They were pleased to see signs of both bear and caribou near their camp—but that was all they saw of the big game.

The peak of Katahdin was the goal on Friday, August 29, and they began their ascent before daybreak. "It was very difficult walking," TR wrote, "and both Emlen and Arthur gave out before reaching the summit, the view from which was beautiful."[14] The hard granite of the mountain is unforgiving to boots with rugged soles, so it's small wonder that Roosevelt felt the going was difficult in his soft-bottom slippers. "I had to do the whole distance in moccasins," he wrote to Bamie, "which protect the feet just about as effectually as kid gloves would. So I got pretty foot sore while climbing the mountain; but nevertheless I was the only one of the three that reached the summit."[15]

The view from the top of Katahdin is intoxicating—a wild fastness trundles off to the horizon in all directions in a rich swirl of green and blue, while your head's in the clouds and the ground seems impossibly far away. Like so many others before and since, TR was reflective when he sat on the summit, and more than a little bit proud of himself for making it there—especially since his cousin and tutor hadn't. "Rather to my surprise, I found I could carry heavier loads and travel farther and faster than either of them; and could stand rough work better,"[16] he'd later recall. Because of the stamina he showed during the climb, Roosevelt saw himself as being cut of the same stuff as the Island Falls men, and for their part they seemed to agree. Sewall would later report: "The stones and crags on the way up cut his feet into tatters. But he kept on, with never a murmur of complaint. That's a little thing, perhaps; but he was that way in all things—always."[17]

On the descent, the group got a bit turned around, which also must have heartened the Harvard student—both of his guides showed they weren't actually superhuman but men who could make mistakes the same as anyone else. "Coming back we followed a spotted trail which sometimes set at fault even the two skilled backwoodsmen,"[18] Roosevelt noted in his diary. They finally made it back to the shore of Katahdin Lake by dark, walking through a soggy afternoon and catching five dozen trout along the way. Tired, footsore, wet, TR was nonetheless quite content, if not exultant. "It is raining and we are all soaked through—" he wrote, "but in excellent health and spirits."[19]

The next morning Roosevelt was off tracking the beasts whose prints he'd seen earlier, walking halfway around the lake but seeing nothing but sign. "Larger game is not scarce but almost impossible to get at," he wrote in frustration.[20] In the afternoon he walked along Sandy Brook and took a duck on Moose Pond.

Camp life was not very comfortable in the wet conditions. "You get pretty dirty in camp," Roosevelt wrote in his diary.[21] He passed Sunday cleaning his guns, mending clothes, and bathing in the lake. "Blackflies have been very numerous this trip," he continued, "and have been a great annoyance to the others; funnily enough they do not bother me very much." He later told Bamie that he wasn't bothered by the insects, but Arthur Cutler was miserable, "his face gradually getting to look like a roughly executed map of the Rocky Mts."[22]

On Monday afternoon the party turned around and began to make its way back to Island Falls. TR went duck hunting that morning in the barrens and bogs near the lake, and that night they made camp near Wassataquoik Stream, the logging waterway where Roosevelt had lost his shoe.

The strenuous work required to backpack for tens of miles at a time across rugged terrain seemed to agree with Roosevelt. "Am in beautiful condition," he wrote. And he continued to compare himself to his companions, marveling at the fact that he could keep up with the Mainers. "I can walk, wrestle, or shoot with most of these lumbermen."[23]

The route home took them back across the East Branch of the Penobscot on foot, and then they climbed into a buckboard and drove the rest of the long way to Island Falls.

After a day of hunting, and a day of preparations in Island Falls, Roosevelt embarked on yet another expedition, this time to the Munsungan Lakes area by boat via the Aroostook River. One of the state's prime logging thoroughfares, the Aroostook is formed by Munsungan and Millinocket streams, starting in the woods north of Katahdin and flowing up to the St. John. Unusual both because it flows north and because of the especially circuitous route it travels, the waterway coursed through a wild wonderland.

This time he planned to travel with Sewall alone, and once again TR was very thorough, listing his provisions in his diary: "I take tea, pork and hardtack and some flour; we have a shelter tent, two blankets, and some cooking utensils; and one complete change of clothing each. I take 50 cartridges for the rifle and 100 for the shotgun. I shall only use moccasins."[24] Either he'd become fond of his moccasins or couldn't get hold of any boots in time for this trip.

Roosevelt and Sewall set off from Island Falls at 5 a.m. on Friday, September 5, headed again to the remote woodlands around the Oxbow, forty-six miles north. There the Aroostook River all but ties itself in a knot, coiling north and south, doubling back as if it were trying to lose itself. Their route took them through "a sparsely settled, thickly wooded country and for about three miles through a dreary waste of burnt land." It took them all day to reach their destination: a "regular backwoods house—fare and sleeping accommodations being both primitive to a degree."[25]

They put their pirogue in on the Aroostook the next morning and ventured about twenty miles up the river, poling most of the way. Roosevelt found the landscape raw and compelling, noting: "The scenery is very beautiful and wild; I saw no trace of man—but also no trace of game. Trout are plenty, however. . . blackflies, mosquitoes, and midges pretty plentiful; I don't mind them much."[26] They stopped before dark to make camp and cook their bread, trout, and partridge.

On Sunday morning they set out early as usual. "Working" and "hunting" on the Sabbath weighed on the earnest Dutch Reformed youth, so, as he put it, he "compromised by not shooting or fishing."[27] For a day of rest, the pair put in a lot of work. They poled upriver until lunchtime, at which point they reached the mouth of Munsungan Stream, finding the water too shallow to be passable. They had to drag their boat a long way, trudging up the stream bed—"the water now up to our ankles, now to our hips. It was heavy work; moreover it was raining heavily; and towards dusk we pitched camp, drenched through and tired out. Midges bad."[28]

The following day was more of the same—wet, cold, hard. The rain came down steadily as they again heaved their boat upstream. "For several hours it was rapid, shoal water, through which we waded, dragging the heavy dug-out over the rocks and shallows."[29] And the difficulties continued to mount—beaver dams, log jams, and a series of cascades blocked the way. Often they'd have to empty the contents of the boat to make it more maneuverable or to portage around a waterfall. Finally, they reached water deep enough to pole, and then they made Little Munsungan Lake. By late afternoon they stopped at middle Munsungan and camped, all but collapsing with exhaustion. In a letter to Bamie, Roosevelt would say, "[W]hen night came we would lie down, drenched through, too tired to care much one way or the other."[30]

Was Bill Sewall testing the boy at this point? He must have known—at least approximately—the hardships they would face. The experienced guide couldn't have predicted the rain, but he surely would have known the landscape and what it took to traverse it. Despite all the challenges—or perhaps because of them—Roosevelt was enjoying himself. "Tired out, and wet through, hungry and cold—but am having a lovely time,"[31] he wrote in his journal.

The rain just kept coming, and on Tuesday the pair paddled Munsungan Lake and then bushwhacked to the head of Chase Lake. TR recorded his sightings: "On the way I saw a few partridges; an old moose track; a recent bear track; and a few old signs of deer and caribou." All this amounted to "scarce" game in his estimation, and he decided to cut the trip short, "coming back a week earlier than I expected, as I found absolutely no large game."[32]

They turned back the next day, rising before the sun and paddling down the chain of lakes. On the return leg, they essentially retraced their steps, only this time, because of all the recent rain, they were able to run a lot of the swift water that they previously had to carry through. By early afternoon they reached the camp they had stayed in on Saturday and they opted to set up there once again. "I am very fond of the evenings round the campfire, beneath the shelter tents," TR affirmed.[33]

During their fireside chats, Roosevelt would often try out ideas on Sewall that had nothing to do with tracking game or poling wilderness waterways. Almost fourteen years separated the two, and the twenty-one-year-old looked up to Sewall for his opinions. "He used to consult me on many things, I being considerably older than he," Sewall told the *Los Angeles Times* after Roosevelt had become governor of New York. "And one day he said to me as we were camping on the Aroostook River: 'Bill, do you know that I've been worrying a good deal since I left you about my future? If I follow my own natural bent I will be a naturalist, for you know how I love nature, the woods, birds and plants and the rough Arab life of the big woods. But do you know, Bill,' said he earnestly, and with a queer look on his boyish face, 'I have decided that perhaps I can be of more active service to my fellow man if I enter public life. I feel that I can do some good in that way which I could not by writing on nature and leading a simple naturalist's life.'"[34] Sewall assured him he could go far as a politician.

The weather improved in the morning, and so did Roosevelt's luck. Under clear skies they continued home and TR bagged a rabbit, a wood duck, and a ruffed grouse. The pair spent much of the day on foot, walking about fifteen miles cross-country until they found another "rough backwoods house,"[35] and camped inside.

The next day took them ten miles to a pond and a cranberry bog, and for their efforts they were rewarded with a black duck, a hawk, and two ruffed grouse. At last, on Saturday, they reached the bustling hamlet of Island Falls, putting in about twenty-five miles on foot. TR was reveling in the countryside—"the scenery beautiful—for besides the forests, grand enough in themselves, we passed several waterfalls in deep ravines."[36] They had covered so much terrain—having put in fifty miles hauling the boat alone—that Roosevelt wore completely through his moccasins and his feet were aching.

Theodore Roosevelt was pleased to settle back into the Sewall House for a little relaxation and conversation, and he felt better getting back to a proper church. Aside from the creature comforts, though, the son of privilege was greatly enjoying the rough-hewn company he was keeping, foreshadowing the populism he'd espouse during his political career. "I always like these backwoods meeting houses," he admitted, "and I don't know a better or more intelligent race of men than the shrewd, plucky, honest, Yankees—all of them hunters, lumbermen or small farmers."[37]

The admiration seemed to go both ways. The Sewalls weren't the only residents of Island Falls to admire TR. "Everyone in the village liked him," Sewall would tell the *Los Angeles Times* twenty years later, "for he was as plain as a spruce board and liked to associate with the common people."[38]

While in the Falls, TR wrote to Bamie, vividly capturing his experience on the Munsungan adventure: "I enjoyed the trip exceedingly, but I think it was the roughest work I have yet had in the way of camping out; our trip to Katahdin was absolute luxury compared to it. . . . You can have no idea what severe labour dragging a boat up a swift mountain stream is: to be in the water up to your hips ten hours at a stretch is in itself hard enough, and this only represents the least part of it."[39]

It wouldn't be long before he was hankering to get back outside. After relaxing for a couple of days, he and Sewall, along with Wilmot Dow, ventured out on Tuesday, and TR's description again raises questions about whether the guide was testing his charge: "Started with Bill, in a rough wagon with a rougher horse; the roads were rougher still; and the cabin we are now staying in, after going about thirty miles, is roughest of all."[40]

A couple of uneventful days hunting followed in the Island Falls area, with Roosevelt bagging but a couple of birds. The vacationing Harvard student wasn't bothered by that or anything else. He was toughening up and delighting in it. "[A]s usual, it rained," he reported, "the weather has been awful for the last two weeks; but I am enjoying myself exceedingly, am in superb health, and as tough as a pine knot."[41]

For the next several days Roosevelt, Sewall, and Dow camped on Mattawamkeag Lake, exploring the surrounding woodlands and shooting just about anything that moved. They routinely put in twenty-mile days and typically took home a few birds each evening. Finding very little game one afternoon, they practiced their marksmanship, and Roosevelt naturally compared himself to his companions. "I shot very well," he wrote in his diary. "But not as well as Dow and Sewall."[42]

The next day the trio paddled back to Island Falls to spend the night, pack up, and head south to meet TR's train. This time the trek to the depot would be a hunting expedition as well, and take them two days and many miles, picking up the train at Kingman Station about ten miles north of Mattawamkeag.

Upon his return to Cambridge, Roosevelt was ebullient, and he seems to have cast off the shadow of his father's death once and for all. "What glorious fun I am having this year!" he exclaimed. "No fellow ever had a better time than I have. And my life has such absurd contrasts. At one time I live in the height of luxury; and then for a month will undergo really severe toil and hardship—and I enjoy both extremes almost equally."[43]

He echoed those sentiments when writing to his mother: "I was really sorry to leave both Sewall and Dow; I have had capital fun this trip, and have passed as pleasant a month as a fellow could. Am feeling as strong as a bull.

"By Jove, it sometimes seems as I were having too happy a time to have it last. I enjoy every moment I live, almost."[44]

For all his elation about his experiences in the North Woods, though, he'd never make it back to Island Falls.

Harvard Cool

U pon his return to Harvard, Theodore Roosevelt couldn't stop talking about his trip to Maine. The trek up Mount Katahdin and especially his adventures in the Munsungan Lakes area seem to have marked another turning point for him. Since he had met Sewall and Dow, he was always comparing himself to them, and, on this visit, he felt he was finally man enough to stand in their company. "I find I can endure fatigue and hardship pretty nearly as well as these lumbermen,"[1] he declared.

Roosevelt was thrilled with this realization. In his own mind, at least, he was on his way to becoming one of them—a rugged, self-sufficient man. It didn't hurt that he had fared better on the stout shoulders of Katahdin than his fellow New Yorkers had. Since his Moosehead Lake epiphany with the bullies in the stage coach, measuring himself against others—his cousins, his brother, his father— had become second nature to him, and he had spent his first years at Harvard comparing himself with his fellow students.[2]

TR was not the only city-bred man concerned about his toughness. Many urban men of this age were worried that they were becoming too soft, too "European." As one twentieth-century writer put it, during Thoreau's time Maine was seen as a "lost happy hunting ground awaiting to cleanse the soul of an age bowing before the false gods of European culture. Boston, New York, Philadelphia; they had all become civilized—'effete' was the word of the day."[3]

Roosevelt saw himself at great risk of being "unmanly" due solely to his upbringing: "Forty or fifty years ago the writer on American morals was sure to deplore the effeminacy and luxury of young Americans who were born of rich parents," he would later write. "The boy who was well off then, especially in the big eastern cities, lived too luxuriously, took to billiards as his chief innocent recreation, and felt small shame in his inability to take part in rough pastimes and field sports."[4] After his time in the Maine woods he felt he had proven himself among the hardest and hardiest of men.

In 1918, looking back on his North Woods experiences, he would acknowledge both his admiration for these Mainers and his eagerness to win their approval. "It was a matter of pride with me to keep up with my stalwart associates," he explained, "and to shift for myself, and to treat with indifference whatever hardship or fatigue came our way. In their company I would have been ashamed to complain!"[5]

Predictably, his friends—even Arthur Cutler—grew tired of hearing the tale of his latest adventure. "It takes Theodore two hours to tell the story of the Munsungan Lake trip," Cutler complained to Sewall in a letter. "And then, after all, it doesn't seem to have amounted to much except a good hard time."[6]

Of course, a good hard time was just what TR needed. His transition to Harvard had been every bit as soft as his boyhood. Bamie had traveled to Cambridge ahead of him and selected a room in a boardinghouse off campus on Winthrop Street—his parents didn't want him in a first-floor dorm due to his asthma. Then she furnished and decorated it for him, and Roosevelt was very grateful. "Ever since I came here," he told her, "I have been wondering what I should have done if you had not fitted up my room for me."[7] This was just more of the same for TR's parents—up to this point they had arranged most aspects of their son's life. When they had packed their boy off to dancing classes in New York, for example, they even drafted the partners to dance with him.[8]

When he entered Harvard, one of the nation's bastions of privilege, he did so as one of its most privileged students, which made adjusting to the new setting all the more difficult. It took Roosevelt the better part of two years to fully settle in. "I enjoy myself ever so much here," he told Bamie in the early days of college, "and the fellows are very pleasant, but I thoroughly realize there's no place like home."[9]

Before he arrived in Cambridge, Roosevelt had never had much in the way of formal schooling. Again because of his asthma, his parents didn't think it appropriate to send him to a public—or even a private—school, so TR missed the day-to-day social interaction that many of his peers experienced. As he put it in his autobiography, "I could not go to school because I knew so much less than most boys of my age in some subjects and so much more in others."[10] To fill in the gaps—Theodore did well in science, history, and geography but he was behind in Latin, Greek, and mathematics—the Roosevelts hired Arthur Cutler in 1873 to tutor their son.

When TR arrived at the nation's oldest university in September of 1876, his classmates didn't know what to make of him. Nor, for that matter, he them. "It is astonishing how few fellows have come here with any idea of getting an education," he wrote Bamie in his first semester.[11] To his father he wrote: "I do not think there is a fellow in college who has a family that love him as much as you do me, and I am sure that there is no one who has a father who is also his best and most intimate friend, as you are mine."[12]

Despite all the working out he'd been doing since the Moosehead Lake incident, TR was still a pale, timid boy during his first year at college—seventeen years old, about five-eight, weighing a slight 124 pounds, and, thanks to those bench presses, boasting a chest measurement of 34 inches.[13] His round face was framed by a pair of long, dark muttonchops, and his thick spectacles made him seem just the library lover he was. A fellow student, whom he met in the gym, referred to him as "a youth in the kindergarten stage of physical development."[14]

Though he had plenty of friends—Roosevelt was particularly close with the wealthy New England Cabots and Saltonstalls of his generation—he was viewed by many of his fellow students, and some professors, as a bit of an odd duck. In his rooms at Winthrop Street he maintainted his habit of keeping a menagerie of animals. One friend, Mark Sullivan, recalled "the excitement caused by a particularly large turtle, sent by a friend from the southern seas, which got out of its box one night and started toward the bathroom in search of water."[15]

There were many at first who had a hard time even pronouncing his name. "Hardly anyone can get my name correctly, except as 'Rosy,'" he grumbled.[16] Thomas Sargent Perry, one of his instructors, called him "bumptious. Not offensively so, by any means, but wearing a certain boyish positiveness."[17]

That particular trait at this particular place and time could be particularly problematic.

The average Harvard student of the era worked to cultivate an air of aloofness, a certain couldn't-care-less attitude. In describing the men of Harvard Yard, the July 1876 issue of *Scribner's Magazine* explained: "That repression or even disdain of enthusiasm, that emulation of high-bred cynicism and arrogant coolness, which in a young man do not be-token the healthiest, strongest character, is prevalent. The divine fervor of enthusiasm is openly, or by implication, voted a vulgar thing."[18] And enthusiasm, of course, was the trait that all but defined Theodore Roosevelt.

The attitude of fashionable aloofness was so ingrained that the school's resident bard, George Pellew, parodied it with an ode to indifference presented at the Hasty Pudding Theater in Roosevelt's senior year:

> We deem it narrow-minded to excel.
> We call the man fanatic who applies
> His life to one grand purpose till he dies.
> Enthusiasm sees one side, one fact;
> We try to see all sides, but do not act. . . .
> We long to sit with newspapers unfurled,
> Indifferent spectators of the world.[19]

Several of TR's classmates thought the young New Yorker simply tried too hard. As his friend John Woodbury would later say, "Roosevelt struck his classmates as unusual. Concentration, enthusiasm. Interest in his studies. He seemed to know what he wanted and was in every way more mature than the rest of his classmates."[20] Another student, Sherrard Billings, recalled that it was exactly this intensity that set him apart: "Roosevelt was striking in college because in a place where men affected indifference he was an enthusiast; where it was not considered good form to move at more than a walk, he was always running."[21]

Running, indeed. Roosevelt took to college like he did most things—with a zeal that bordered on the manic. He was like a fly on a windowscreen, constantly buzzing. "At half past seven my scout, having made the fire and blacked the boots, calls me, and I get round to breakfast at 8," he wrote in one letter home,[22] and from then until the wee hours he was constantly on the go. He had his schoolwork, of course, and the lengthy list of clubs and organizations to which he belonged. He was a member of the Natural History Society, naturally. But he also belonged to the art club, the rifle club, and the finance club. He was an editor of the *Harvard Advocate*, and he took a role in a comedy production. Somehow he still found time to do his schoolwork and win election to Phi Beta Kappa—and to woo Alice Hathaway Lee, who lived all the way across town in Chestnut Hill.

Like Roosevelt, Harvard at the time was in transition. New president Charles Eliot, young and full of ideas, wanted to update the very traditional institution and turn it into a "modern" university. While it enjoyed a reputation as a fine school, it was also viewed as a place concerned as much with athletics and social skills as it was with academics. A story in the *Boston Saturday Evening Gazette*, published in November of Roosevelt's senior year, said as much: "The chief distinctions achieved by a certain class of Harvard students, during the past few years, have been in connection with baseball, boat racing, bicycling, and other sporting accomplishments in which brawn comes to the fore and the brain retires in the background. In fact, this 'description' of [the] Harvard student, as he makes himself most familiar to the public, is an immature being, more gifted with brawn than with brains. His profoundest aspiration, next to his desire to appear a full-grown man, seems to run in the direction of muscular accomplishment."[23]

As someone zealously attempting to remake himself into a man of action, this glorification of brawn was fine with Roosevelt. He participated in many intramural athletics and enjoyed testing his growing strength against that of other boys. He did a lot of boxing and wrestling in the lightweight divisions at Harvard, but none too successfully. "[I] never attained to the first rank in either, even at my own weight,"[24] he wrote in his autobiography. One apocryphal tale has Roosevelt "administering of a thorough and scientific drubbing to a fellow student, larger and more muscular than himself,"[25] but it appears to be just that.

He wasn't naturally gifted at any athletics or the outdoorsy pursuits he was so drawn to, and he readily admitted as much: "I was fond of horseback-riding, but I took to it slowly and with difficulty, exactly as with boxing. It was a long time before I became even a respectable rider, and I never got much higher."[26]

This was why his ability to shift for himself with Sewall and Dow in the Maine woods meant so much to the young man.

When he entered Harvard, Theodore Roosevelt was as certain as a young college student could be about what he wanted to do with his life—work in natural history or biology. He had even come to an agreement with his father on the subject.

His father could see where his son's interests lay—only a fool would miss it—and during TR's freshman year, he had a long talk with him. He wanted the boy to know that if he was serious about being a scientist, he would support him wholeheartedly. He didn't want his son to choose another line of work solely for financial reasons. But neither did he want him to coast or take advantage of his position—he'd have to work at it. There would be no bankrolling a dilettante. And his father made sure he understood that pockets would not be overflowing with cash. To his way of thinking, he explained, if one isn't making a lot of money from his own industry, he can't be spending a lot of money. If young Theodore became a naturalist instead of a businessman, he'd have to be a thrifty one.[27]

This didn't faze TR a bit. "After this conversation I fully intended to make science my life work," he later wrote. It did not take long to discover that his professors didn't have the same epic view of natural history that he did. "At the time, Harvard, and I suppose our other colleges, utterly ignored the possibilities of the faunal naturalist and observer of nature," he later explained in his autobiography. "They treated biology as purely a science of the laboratory and the microscope."[28]

Working in a basement lab in a stiff white coat was the last thing Theodore Roosevelt wanted to do. "I had no more desire or ability to be a microscopist and section-cutter than to be a mathematician."[29] To TR, the wonders of science—its future and frontiers—were out in the fields and forests and sea awaiting discovery. That's where he wanted to be.

If not science, though, then what? Roosevelt found himself unsure what he wanted to do with his life, for the first time adrift. From his days as a toddler he had been consumed with a passion for natural history, and now he didn't know if he wanted to continue. For an individual as focused and goal-oriented as TR, this uncertainty caused more than a little anxiety.

And then his world imploded.

Theodore Roosevelt, Sr., began having stomach pains while TR was in his freshman year. The elder Roosevelt never said a word to his son about his discomfort, not wanting to trouble him while he was studying. Bamie, however, wrote to TR about the situation, telling him that their father was having some difficulties. And, of course, the boy was concerned. He wrote back to her in December, "I am very uneasy about Father. Did the doctor think it anything serious?"[30] A few lines later, as though he grasped the gravity of the situation, he added, "We have been very fortunate, Bamie, in having a father whom we can love and respect more than any other man in the world."[31]

Their father's pain was caused by a malignant gastrointestinal tumor, which was incurable and grew steadily. He passed away in early February of 1878. Because of the tumor's position, his physicians had not dared to operate. "The symptoms at the last," according to the *New York World*, "were similar to those produced by strangulation of the intestines." Though the doctors understood the fatal nature of the senior Roosevelt's disease, it was not explained to his children. Many in the family attributed the illness to time he spent climbing the mountains of Mount Desert Island during a stay at Bar Harbor with Bamie in the summer of 1877. Somehow, they suggested, he "strained himself" on one of these vigorous hikes.[32]

During his last few weeks, Theodore senior's wife, his daughters, his youngest son, and various aunts and uncles all watched over him, along with the family servants. Everyone but TR, who was off at college and to a certain extent unaware of the dire nature of the illness. When he'd been home for Christmas his father seemed to be on the mend; then just a few weeks later he received an urgent telegram to return to New York at once. He arrived too late for a final farewell.

His family as a whole took the loss of their patriarch extremely hard. Bamie and Conie were crushed. Some say Elliott never was quite the same afterward.[33] And TR told his friend Harry Minot, "Father had always been so much with me that it seems as if part of my life had been taken away."[34]

Roosevelt returned to Harvard a vacant shell, and poured his sadness and anguish into his journals. When his grief overwhelmed him, as it did repeatedly, he wrote to Bamie for support: "I feel that if it were not for the certainty, that as he himself has so often said, 'He is not dead but gone before,' I should almost perish. With the help of my God I will try to lead such a life as he would have wished."[35]

Sadness often led to self doubt. One day during church he had a particular fit of worthlessness: "During service today I could not help reflecting sadly on how little use I am, or ever shall be in the world . . . . I realize more and more every day that I am as much inferior to Father morally and mentally as I am physically."[36]

His father's death created another natural vacuum in his life—the elder Roosevelt had been his son's chief advisor and principal male role model. He would have helped him work through his options when he decided against natural history. "Oh Father, Father, no words can tell how I shall miss your counsel and your advice,"[37] he anguished.

It was in this context and in this state of mind that eight months after his father's death, TR traveled north to Island Falls for the first time.

Playing the Frontier

He first met her on October 18, 1878, little more than month after he first met Bill Sewall. A flirtatious beauty with perfect golden brown curls and bright gray-blue eyes, Alice Hathaway Lee lived next door to one of TR's best friends, Dick Saltonstall, in Chestnut Hill. She was almost three years younger than Roosevelt and shared several of the traits of his mother, according to many at the time.[1] When she was young, her family had called her "Sunshine" because of her warm disposition,[2] and like TR she had a zeal for life. He was captivated the very first time he saw her and remained so throughout his college career. Though he would mention any number of girls to Bamie during his Harvard years—Miss Richardson, Miss Fiske, Miss Elsie Burnett, Miss Madeleine Mixter, Miss Lulu Lane, Miss Jeannie Hooper, Miss Bessie Whitney—one name began to win out after November 1878.[3]

Theodore Roosevelt became as serious about wooing Alice as he was about anything else he set his mind to, and brought his characteristic enthusiasm to the chase. "See that girl?" he told a woman at a Hasty Pudding event, "I am going to marry her. She won't have me, but I am going to have *her*."[4]

Roosevelt spent the last two years of college in full chase. Alice completely intrigued him, and he all but beatified her: "She is so radiantly good and pure and beautiful that I almost feel like worshiping her."[5] There were nights that he wandered through the woods of Boston trying to come to terms with his obsession, which prompted friends to write home to his family, suggesting that someone come up to make sure he wasn't losing it.[6] He'd given himself over to her completely, even asking her to marry him in June of 1879.[7] "She shall always be mistress over all that I have,"[8] he wrote in his diary.

And she was. Though he seemed too anxious to notice, and perhaps she too flirtatious to fully reveal it, Alice was completely taken by his attentions. The couple spent as much time together as possible and as was acceptable. They covered tens of miles in walks together, she being just as willing and able as he to "clamber over fences."[9] They went to dinners and dances, and even snuck into the Porcellian Club, which did not admit women.[10] When TR successfully trapped a lynx in the Mattawamkeag area during his second trip to Island Falls, he had the pelt made into a rug for Alice.

In February 1880, Alice Hathaway Lee finally consented to marry TR. That June Roosevelt graduated magna cum laude from Harvard, ranking twenty-first in his class of 177.[11] And a few weeks later the engaged couple were off with friends to Mount Desert Island along the coast of Maine. Alice and her friend Rose Saltonstall stayed with a family in Bar Harbor proper, while TR and Dick Saltonstall set up at the home of another chum, Jack Tebbetts, on Schooner Head, a rugged little curve of coastline sticking out into Frenchman Bay south of town. Every day Roosevelt would make the three-mile round trip back to Bar Harbor to be with Alice. They'd bowl, play tennis, stroll the Shore Path, and enjoy the "perfectly magnificent scenery."[12]

This was the beginning of Bar Harbor's golden age, and summer sojourns there were much in vogue for the rich and famous of the East. It was also the place where the Roosevelt family believed Theodore Roosevelt, Sr., first began to suffer from the illness that killed him, overexerting himself on climbs of area peaks. This didn't stop his son from doing the same, despite the fact that he'd been warned away from strenuous activity by a physician a few months before.

In March, Roosevelt had been seen by the Harvard doctor, a routine exam given to graduating students. His measurements were much the same as they had been four years prior, when he was a freshman, except that he now weighed a dozen pounds more. The doctor had pulled him aside and issued him a warning. As Bill Sewall would recount later, the doctor told Roosevelt that his heart was weak and cautioned him to seek some sort of profession that didn't require strenuous work, as even such stress as running up the stairs could prove fatal.[13]

Sewall liked the story. "Well, he said to that man: 'Now doctor, I am going to do all the things that you have told me not to do, for if I had to live a life such as you have pictured to me, I wouldn't care how short my life was.'"[14]

And here he was in Bar Harbor, playing tennis in the morning and climbing mountains in the afternoon. Alice and TR spent the better part of three weeks that August gallivanting around the seaside playground. True to form, TR took sick. This time it was a few days of "cholera morbus," the nineteenth-century term for acute gastroenteritis. He'd been afflicted with it before.[15]

Only a week later, Roosevelt was aboard a train with his brother Elliott heading west. At the time, the Great Plains were considered prime hunting territory. It was still the Wild West of legend, the final frontier of North America, and held a romantic allure not only for the Roosevelts but for many an Easterner.

The brothers were going ostensibly to hunt, but they were also strongly encouraged by their family to visit their cousin Jack Elliott, who lived on the Red River in Moorehead, Minnesota, just across from Fargo. Off they went to see him, perched right on the edge of the unorganized Dakota Territory and the plains of the Sioux, a land of buffalo below and a sea of sky above.[16] The two brothers spent weeks hunting the prairie, guided by locals, sleeping in shacks and under the stars, and between them they bagged 404 animals, including snipe, grouse, plovers, and geese.[17]

Simply getting out with a firearm got the testosterone flowing. Roosevelt wrote to Bamie: "We have had three days good shooting and I feel twice the man for it already."[18] The raw, wide-open country seemed to agree with his cousin, too. Roosevelt couldn't help noticing that Jack seemed much the same as he was when they were young, but "more of a man and really good looking." They had a fine time—TR proclaiming himself "in superb health."[19]

The rest of the summer was spent romancing and preparing for the biggest event in TR's young life. As reported one Saturday in October 1880, in the *Brookline Chronicle Saturday*: "There was a fashionable wedding at the First Parish Church, on Wednesday of this week, contracting parties being Miss Alice H. daughter of George C. Lee, Esq., of Chestnut Hill, and Mr. Theodore Roosevelt, of New York. The Rev. J.A. Buckingham performed the ceremony. The reception was held at the residence of the bride's parents in the evening."[20] The couple were married on Roosevelt's twenty-second birthday. After a honeymoon at the familiar haunt on Oyster Bay, they moved in with TR's mother at West 57th Street in New York.

The last four years at Harvard and in the Maine woods, and winning Alice's hand in marriage, had given Theodore Roosevelt a new confidence. He was no longer a boy. Even so, he remained unsure what he wanted to pursue as a career. Having given up natural history, he thought perhaps law made sense. To test the waters, he took a job working in his Uncle Robert's firm while studying law at Columbia, and he found that the work suited him well. He got his start in politics at this time, too, being elected in November 1881 to the first of three one-year terms in the New York State Assembly. Continuing his quest to be his father's son, he became a trustee of the Orthopedic Hospital and the New York Infant Asylum and also joined or started a variety of other fraternal or social organizations.

One of these organizations was the Free Trade Club, where in May 1883 Roosevelt made the acquaintance of Henry Gorringe, a retired naval officer. The pair got to talking—Roosevelt had been working on a book of naval history since Harvard—and Gorringe mentioned to him that he had purchased property in the Badlands. He was going to turn an abandoned army post into a hunting lodge. Having had a taste of the West, Roosevelt was intrigued, and Gorringe invited him out to the Dakota territory.

The West of the 1880s was still a wild land in the popular imagination where a man could capitalize on the many untapped resources, if he had the stomach for it. Like Maine's North Woods, it was just the sort of untamed place that was rich dream fodder for Roosevelt. Gorringe's project no doubt fed his appetite for derring-do, coupling it with the tantalizing excitement of almost certain profits. Ultimately Gorringe had to back out of the expedition, but, ever eager, Roosevelt decided he would go anyway. At the very least, he wanted to bag a buffalo before they were all gone.[21]

Roosevelt and his friend were hardly alone in seeing dollar signs on the prairie. Books like James Brisbin's *The Beef Bonanza: Or, How to Get Rich on the Plains*, published in 1881, were adding to the mystique of ranch life. According to a study of the range and ranch business conducted by Congress: "The opportunities for gain and the wild fascination of the herdsman's life has [sic] drawn to Texas many young men of education and fortune in the northern states and even scions of noble families in Europe. This has also been the case throughout the entire range and cattle ranch area of the United States."[22]

It was estimated that, during 1884, about 300,000 head of cattle were driven from Texas to the "northern ranges," which would have included the Dakotas, to be fattened up for market. In 1884 the Northern Pacific Railroad delivered 90,000 head to the Dakotas and Montana to stock new ranches. There was so much excitement about the cattle industry that the Native Americans were increasingly losing their lands to ranchers. According to E.V. Smalley of St. Paul, Minnesota, in an appendix to the Congressional report, "more territory will be opened by reduction of the large Indian reservations in Dakota and Montana."[23]

With all this in mind, Theodore Roosevelt boarded the train for the Dakota Badlands in early September of 1883. Part of the appeal of the Dakotas for Roosevelt was the relative ease of access. At five days, it took longer but it was simpler to get to than even Island Falls: Take the train from New York to St. Paul, hop onto the Northern Pacific Railroad and ride a few more trains to the small outpost of Little Missouri in Dakota Territory. No long days on a buckboard over bumpy roads. Ride in comfort, read and work, then step off the platform in Little Missouri, and you were in the Badlands.

On the trip he wrote his "Darling Motherling" from Bismarck: "Although I have traveled steadily since I left New York, and have spent four nights in the cars, yet I feel perfectly fresh and well, especially as I have just had a good bath and shave."[24]

Roosevelt spent his first night at the "ramshackle" Pyramid Park Hotel in Little Missouri, some 130 miles west of Bismarck. The accommodations were worth writing home about: "I reached here last night at two, and got into the 'hotel' with some difficulty; there I was given a bed in a room with eight other gentlemen, all of more or less doubtful aspect. However, I slept well."[25]

The next day, he took off for the army base his friend Gorringe had told him about. He also contracted the services of a local guide, Joe Ferris, to take him bison hunting. He and Ferris would travel to Chimney Butte Ranch, the cattle operation Ferris ran with his brother, Sylvane, and his business partner, William Merrifield. Just outside Medora, Dakota, the ranch house itself was primitive by Roosevelt's standards—one room, dirt floor, cookstove, three bunks.

But Roosevelt was already as smitten with the lifestyle and livelihood of the Badlands as he had been with the vast forests of Maine. Even more so. "I do not believe there ever was any life more attractive to a vigorous young fellow than life on a cattle ranch in those days," he insisted. "I enjoyed the life to the full."[26]

He spent ten days on the buffalo hunt with Ferris, and then stayed on with a father-and-son pair of Scottish immigrants, Gregory and Lincoln Lang, who had a place on the Cannonball River. Lincoln would later recall his father and TR staying up late at night to discuss ranching and hunting and politics: "[I]t was listening to those talks after supper in the old shack on the Cannonball that I first came to understand that the Lord made the earth for all of us and not just for the chosen few."[27]

When Roosevelt wasn't hunting or helping with ranch chores, he spent time poking around the area and exploring Medora. In a letter home, he described it as "a typical frontier town of the northwest; go-ahead, prosperous, and unfinished; the original log cabins and tents have been almost entirely supplanted by frame houses; and there are a number of pretentious brick buildings going up. The streets are crowded with frontiersmen; rough looking but quiet farmers, American, Scandinavian, or German; cowboys, on shaggy horses; with gaily decked saddles; saturnine hunters, lounging about with long rifles; and squalid, fierce looking Indians; all combined make a very picturesque appearance. The town stands in the midst of a limitless, treeless expanse of rolling prairie, broken only to the southwest by the forests on the edge of the mighty Missouri, beyond which the bluffs rise in grim nakedness."[28]

He could see the business possibilities here, and he was keenly interested. The Northern Pacific Railroad connected the growing community to the cities to the east—Bismarck, Fargo, St. Paul—and the infrastructure for the cattle business was already being developed. It was a place where you could still buy in early and position yourself to profit as the town and the industry grew.

After spending ten days on the hunt with Ferris, Roosevelt decided he didn't want to leave. Or rather, that he wanted a more permanent piece of this lifestyle.

TR himself recognized the element of youthful wish fulfillment involved in his attraction to the West. In a letter to Bamie he admitted as much: "I have been fulfilling a boyish ambition of mine—that is, I have been playing the frontier hunter in good and earnest."[29] And TR being TR, he played it to the hilt, working hard to look the part. Riding the range or strolling the streets of Medora, he affected a "sombrero, silk neckerchief, riding trousers, a buckskin shirt, boots of alligator leather and carried pearl hilted revolvers and a Winchester rifle." He found that the buckskin not only made him feel like his heroes Davy Crockett, Daniel Boone, and Sam Houston, but it was practical, too, making his movements quieter and more difficult for wildlife to detect. The trophy room at Oyster Bay began filling up as he shipped home elk heads and bear skins and sheep horns.

Many of the hardscrabble ranchmen he met were unsure what to make of this Eastern dude with his brand-new cowboy getup. His eyeglasses and high voice put off some, as did his unflagging enthusiasm and fancy pedigree. Naturally, some saw his buckskins as an affectation and Theodore Roosevelt as a rank dilettante. Both Joe and Sylvane Ferris remembered their first impressions of their guest. "The day Mr. Roosevelt came up to our ranch," recalled Sylvane, "he looked just like any other eastern man. Didn't pay much attention to him. He wore large glasses that made him look funny out there."[30]

"He struck me as being a pretty nice fellow in those days," Joe Ferris recalled. "Didn't have much to say to anybody, quiet sort of fellow. He had those big glasses on and [they] made him look kinda odd to us fellows out there who wasn't used to those things on, but he impressed me from the first as being a mighty nice fellow."[31]

The editor of the local *Badlands Cowboy* newspaper wasn't quite as generous: "Mr. Roosevelt is still at Ferris and Merrifield's ranch hunting and playing cowboy. It seems to be more congenial work than reforming New York politics. . . . He is thoroughly inspired with the profit of raising cattle in the Badlands, as his vigorous backing of Ferris Bros. and Merrifield testifies."[32]

Roosevelt was so thoroughly inspired that he returned to the Dakotas in 1884 and paid a visit to the offices of the *Badlands Cowboy* to explain his new idea—setting up his own ranch under the management of two men he was sure would make fine cowboys, Bill Sewall and Wilmot Dow from the State of Maine. He'd locate his lash-up thirty-five miles north of Medora because the land nearer to town and to the railroad was already being bought up.

He knew just the spot. During one of his previous explorations of the area, he had happened upon a particular bend in the Little Missouri that he found appealing. There was a cottonwood grove down by the river, hills soaring all around, and on the site he'd found a pair of elk antlers locked together as if the animals had been in full combat. This, he decided, would be the lucky place to plant his roots.[33]

Light Comes In; Light Goes Out

L ike Medora, the frontier town of Island Falls was continuing to grow, thanks in large part to the Sewalls. Bill's logging business was prospering, the town had almost two hundred residents by the early 1880s, and across the street from the Sewall House, Charles Berry built the community's first store.

Sewall was working in the woods and wondering how TR was faring. He'd heard from Roosevelt that he'd gone to Europe and was climbing in the Alps. As the guide told a *Los Angeles Times* reporter years later: "He said that some Englishmen at his hotel were bragging that there wasn't an American in Switzerland who had spunk enough to climb the Matterhorn; 'and,' said he, 'I just went out and did it to spite them.'"[1]

The life of the new Harvard grad was a whirlwind, and he didn't have time to make it back to The County. The *L.A. Times* reporter quoted Sewall as saying, "He didn't come one year, and I never felt so lonely in my life," and remarking that when Roosevelt announced his impending marriage, "I feared he would forget his old friend of the woods way down east."[2] He needn't have worried; Roosevelt was not the sort to forget friends, and Sewall wouldn't be lonesome for long.

In 1879, Mary Alice Sherman moved to Island Falls from Oakfield, eight miles to the north, to help her sister, Susan, run the Berry store. Charles Berry, Susan's husband, had fallen ill, and she also needed help with their four children. A tiny thing at five-foot-two, with long, dark hair and dark, deepset eyes, Mary had been born in Salisbury, in the eastern reaches of New Brunswick, Canada, and moved with her mother and father, a lumberman, to Aroostook County when she was three. She arrived in Island Falls around Thanksgiving and met the Sewalls right off, though it wasn't until after Christmas that she spent any time with Bill. Aware that Charles Berry wasn't well, Sewall dropped by the Berrys' one afternoon to take a bunch of the Berry children ice fishing on the river. When one of the youngest boys pleaded to tag along as well, Sewall allowed as how that would be fine—if Mary would come along to watch him. They spent the day together, even though they'd filled their fish buckets within the first hour.

Mary settled into the community easily, but she had one frustration: she wanted to attend the weekly Island Falls dances, but it was considered very bad form for a young lady to go alone. Some of the local girls went by themselves anyway, but Mary was too proud to show up unescorted. She confided her frustration to a friend within earshot of one of her little nephews, and like many a big-mouth little boy, he blabbed, promptly running right over to the Sewall House and telling everyone how Mary wished someone would take her to the dance. Bill, fifteen years older than Mary, encouraged his nephew, George, to ask her—which he did, several times. Word quickly swirled around town that Mary was the best dancer in Island Falls.

Bill continued to come by and take the Berry kids out on adventures—fiddleheading, fishing, berrying, whatever the season offered—and Mary often went along to help watch the children. Years later, in her memoir, she described how Sewall often spoke to these boys as if they were adults, talking about history and poetry and his friend Theodore Roosevelt, who made up for his weak body with his strong mind and competitive spirit.[3]

Was Sewall generous with his time because he was intrigued by this comely newcomer to Island Falls? Perhaps. Thirty-three-year-old Bill Sewall was considered to be the village's most eligible bachelor, handsome, owner of his own business, heir to his father's house and lands. But he was picky, and many of the available girls in the community had concluded that he wasn't interested in marriage. The joke around town was that the Sewall women considered William too good for any other female. Mary had heard people commenting on what a wonderful husband Bill Sewall would make, yet he never courted anyone and seemed to prefer the company of his sister Sarah.[4]

Mary Sherman was certainly interested, though. She was quite taken with the quiet guide. As her biographer put it, she saw him as a transplanted Viking, tall and blond, with strikingly blue eyes. She found him handsome and was impressed by his stature in the community.[5] When he was in the woods logging or off in Houlton or elsewhere on business trips, she found she missed him. Once, when she bumped into him on the street, she was quietly thrilled that he complimented her on a dress she had just sewn. Soon the people of Island Falls were talking about how much time Mary Sherman was spending at the dances and with Bill Sewall.

Charles Berry's illness proved incurable, and the two sisters increasingly found themselves with a household and business to run and no man to help them do it. Among the things they had to do without were skates for the three kids, until Bill Sewall showed up one day with four pairs so the Berry boys—and Mary, too—could join the other village children on the ice.

The skating parties became a regular occurrence, and the little Berrys often jockeyed to see who got to whirl around on the ice with Aunt Mary. On one particular afternoon while they were doing so, Bill Sewall cut in, saying something to the effect of "It's my turn now," as he took Mary's hand. She found him to be the best skater on the ice, strong and graceful. He was just as impressed with her.[6]

A week later the tall woodsman asked for her hand in marriage.

Sewall was working at his woodpile the day after he proposed and Mary was outside doing chores when he called her over. She asked how he was doing, and he confessed that he felt much more at ease around her now that his intentions were out in the open.[7]

They planned the wedding for New Year's Day 1883, so it wouldn't interfere with Thanksgiving or Christmas events, and set the time at 8 p.m. to allow them to get a full day's work in beforehand. The ceremony would take place in the parlor of the Sewall House. Modest as their plans were, they did arrange for a band from Sherman to come and serenade them. The local justice of the peace, George Donham, would preside.

Mary admired the cultured, open nature of the Sewall household, though with her nuptials impending, she fretted about how she would fit in.[8] Their parlor was the finest room she'd even been in.[9] The Sewalls had always welcomed her as warmly as they did all their guests, but did they really approve of their beloved son marrying a poor girl from Oakfield?

On the day of the wedding, bride and groom again met in the street. When Sewall doffed his hat and complimented Mary on how beautiful she looked, her sister burst out laughing—Mary, who was bringing in firewood at the time, was wearing a ratty old sweater. If he thought Mary looked good then, wait until he saw her tonight, she told her future brother-in-law.[10]

Turning to go, Sewall, the ever-practical woodsman, told Mary to come on over when she was ready for the wedding. She stared at him, incredulous at his nonchalance, then stretched herself to her full five-foot, two-inch height and replied that there would be no wedding unless he harnessed up the horse and came for her in his sleigh.[11]

He arrived at 7:30 p.m., reins in hand.

The Sewall House was decorated with cedar boughs, and the place was filled with people—Bill's mother, Rebecca, his sister Sarah, brothers Dave and Sam and their wives, various nieces and nephews, and many friends. Because of the bitter cold, the band from Sherman couldn't get their instruments to play, so they never even started for Island Falls. But the evening was a success nonetheless, and people lingered long into the night to celebrate the new couple, catch up with their neighbors, and avoid the cold outside.

The day after he was married, Sewall resumed his work in the woods, rising early and pulling on his boots. When Mary later expressed curiosity about what went on at the job site, Bill took her along for a day. He fashioned a little lean-to out of cut boughs and made a fire for her to sit by while he and his crew cut trees. As Mary's biographer would later write, she was "so happy in the clear air," that she had a "wonderful day."[12]

Of course, the lumbering life was not always so sweet and picturesque. It was difficult and dirty and fraught with dangers—from simple exposure to the elements to broken limbs to death by crushing or drowning. Bill Sewall saw his share of casualties, and his name would travel farther and wider after one particularly near-death incident.

His crew was moving the last of their logs down the Mattawamkeag River just above the falls, and Sewall had just taken off his caulks to have lunch at home when his mother rushed out onto the porch and pointed at the river. Sewall turned to see a man clinging to a log in the middle of the rushing rapids. It appeared as though he'd planned to land on a bank above the falls but had miscalculated the current. It was one of their neighbors, Ed Hillman.

"He'll go over the falls, won't he? He'll be drowned, won't he?" Mrs. Sewall asked.

"I think so," replied Bill. "For he can't swim."

Sewall could tell he wouldn't be able to be of any help to Hillman before the falls, but he threw his boots back on and sprinted for the river below the falls. When he reached the site he could see the man's head. Then his feet. Then his head—he was still holding onto the rolling log, "an exceedingly dangerous predicament for a man who can't swim," Sewall later noted.

Because he knew the river well, Sewall knew just the point to intercept Hillman. He made for a ledge that sloped down to the water, and right opposite the bank there was a long log that had fetched up and was sticking out into the stream like a breakwater. Sewall used it as a diving board, running its length and leaping out toward the approaching log. Within a few strokes he grabbed the floating timber and pulled himself onto it.

"When I reached him, I asked him if he could hold onto the log if I could keep it from rolling," the woodsman recounted. "He answered that he could." So Sewall steadied the log and steered it around as many obstacles as he could—strainers and rocks—until Hillman told him he could no longer hang on. Sewall then swung to the back of the log, reached over it, and grabbed the struggling man.

By this time other men were running alongshore, following the floating log downstream. One hearty-looking fellow with a pickpole ran out onto a log jam to snag the errant timber and pull it and its two occupants into the eddy. "As we went by he gave the log a tremendous thrust," Sewall recalled. "But in his excitement, he had somehow gotten hold of a pole that had no pike in it." In other words, the pole was missing the barbed hook needed to securely latch onto the log. Hillman and his rescuer sped past.

Sewall shouted to other men running along the riverbank to swim toward them with poles and tug them to shore. None heeded his call, however—they knew the water was fast and cold.

Then Sewall spotted two men shoving off in a boat. The man in the bow was leaning out as they approached, but just then the small craft hit a rock, sending him over the rail into the water. "They'll be too late," Hillman moaned, and the log-bound pair splashed by before the man in the stern could pull his fellow paddler back in.

Hillman's weak voice reminded Sewall that time was running out. Luckily, another shoreside group was readying a bateau and, despite dumping one of their number in the shallows, were able to position the boat downsteam of the surging log and intercept it. Sewall helped to heave Hillman over the gunwale and then quickly followed. "It didn't take me long to get into the boat," he commented.

Typical of Sewall, after making certain his neighbor would revive, he walked back home and set out to finish the day as if nothing had happened. "I judge we had been in the water about half an hour," he recalled. "I changed my clothes, ate my custard, which was still waiting for me, and started back to work." When he got back, the man who had hired him and his crew told him to take the day off, saying that he was "well satisfied with what I had done, even if I didn't do anything else that spring." Sewall put in a full afternoon anyway and actually stayed late that night.[13]

Like any new bride, it took the newest Sewall some time to adjust to her new home. Though Bill's sister Sarah "accepted her completely" into the clan, Mary continued to have doubts about her place in the Sewall House. She suspected that "Mrs. Sewall did not wholeheartedly approve of her,"[14] but she never discussed it with anyone.

Other than that anxiety, though, Mary loved the window the Sewall House gave her on the wider world. This came both from her husband's unending quest for knowledge and from the many guests who stayed with them. Bill was keenly interested in the goings-on beyond the limits of Island Falls. He read the newspaper daily, and both he and Mary regularly visited the community library, which was in Dave Sewall's house, on the hunt for new books. (Unfortunately, these were "still rare," according to Mary.) Whenever guest speakers would give talks in Island Falls, Bill and Mary were in the audience.[15]

Many interesting people came right to their home. Everyone looking for lodging in Island Falls made it to the Sewall House. As long as they behaved themselves, didn't drink or smoke or become rowdy, Bill Sewall would do whatever he could to provide for them. He enjoyed hearing from these travelers about goings on elsewhere. Mary and her sister-in-law never knew when another bed or another place at the table would be needed. With all the work of running the house, neither had much time for talk, but sometimes in the evenings Mary could sit down with the visitors and shed her weariness as she listened to stories of Bangor and Portland, Boston, New York and Washington, Chicago and San Francisco.[16]

Bill Sewall reveled in these conversations, and he was ever pleased to show off the community they were building. Many men and women in Island Falls possessed a pioneer spirit and a sense of optimism about the town's future, but Mary thought her new husband personified that local pride more than anyone else.[17]

And, of course, Mary heard all about Sewall's favorite New Yorkers, especially Theodore Roosevelt. The guide still received regular letters from his peripatetic friend, telling him of his hunts and travels, his love for Alice, and his entrance into politics. Sewall watched from afar as Roosevelt was elected to the New York state senate three times and quickly gained fame for his anti-corruption stance.

Roosevelt's political ambitions were rising, but his party was slipping away from him, or so he thought. On a national level, the Republicans had nominated James G. Blaine, of Maine, to stand as their candidate for president. TR was from the more progressive wing of the party and had actively opposed Blaine's candidacy. The man from Maine had a tarnished reputation, and many of Roosevelt's closest friends and colleagues steadfastly refused to support him. Though TR shared their opinion of Blaine, he stood by his party's nominee. His loyalty lost him some friends, and the world of politics started to lose its appeal.

He said as much in an April 1884 letter to the editor of the *Utica Morning Herald*: "I have very little expectation of being able to keep on in my politics. . . I doubt if any man can realize the bitter and venomous hatred with which I am regarded by the very politicians who at Utica supported me."

The whole matter had him thinking of taking a break from government for a while, perhaps heading back to Maine. "For very many reasons I will not mind going back into private [life] for a few years," he wrote. "My work this winter has been very harrassing. . . . I think I shall spend the next two or three years in making shooting trips either in the Far West or the Northern Woods."[18]

Things were only going to get worse. That winter, Sewall received a letter than hit him hard. As the woodsman later recounted, "It was during Theodore's third term in the legislature, in February 1884, that his daughter Alice was born. That very night his mother, who had been an invalid for years, died suddenly, and twelve hours later his wife also died. Cutler wrote me about it: 'Theodore's mother died on Thursday morning at 3 a.m. His wife died the same day at 10 a.m., about twenty-four hours after the birth of his daughter. Of course, the family are utterly demoralized and Theodore is in a dazed, stunned state. He does not know what he does or says.... The funeral of both Mrs. Roosevelts took place this morning. A very sad sight. The legislature has adjourned for three days out of respect for Theodore's loss.'"[19]

Alice had given Roosevelt "three years of happiness greater and unalloyed than I have ever known," as he wrote in his diary, and now she was gone, a casualty of a kidney malady known as Bright's disease. He was inconsolable, a wreck. The day is marked in his diary with a black X. A couple of days later he noted simply: "The light has gone out of my life." Two days after that: "for joy or sorrow, my life has now been lived out."[20]

The news cast a pall over the Sewall household. Bill felt his friend's pain so deeply that he focused on it for days.[21] He wrote to Roosevelt expressing his sympathies, and about a month later received another letter, this time from Roosevelt himself:

> Dear Will—I was glad to hear from you, and I know you feel for me. It was a grim and evil fate, but I have never believed it did any good to flinch or yield from any blow nor does it lighten the blow to cease from working.
>
> I have thought often of you. I hope my western venture turns out well. If it does, and I feel sure you will do well for yourself by coming out with me, I shall take you and Will Dow out next August. Of course, it depends upon how the cattle have gotten through the winter. The weather has been very hard and I am afraid they have suffered somewhat; if the loss has been very heavy I will have to wait a year longer before going into a more extended scale. So, as yet, the plan is doubtful. If you went out, the first year you could not expect to do very well, but after that, I think, from what I know of you, you would have a very good future before you.
>
> Good-by, dear friend. May God bless you and yours.
>
> Yours always, Theodore Roosevelt[22]

While Sewall was feeling for his friend, he had his own matters of life and death to think about. He and Mary were expecting their first child in April, and his Aunt Deborah Macomber died a few weeks after this letter arrived from Roosevelt. One of her last wishes was to have her remains taken back to Illinois and buried beside those of her husband and the rest of her family. Bill set aside a few weeks to fulfill this request, and he planned to stop in New York on his way home. Roosevelt had written him again at the end of March, telling him he "must take dinner with me if possible" when he was in town. "I have much to talk over with you."[23]

As the guide later described his visit, "I went down to New York that spring to see him and talk things over. He said he would guarantee us a share of anything made in the cattle business, and if anything was lost, he said he would lose it and pay our wages. He asked what I thought of the proposition. I told him that I thought that it was very one-sided but that if he thought he could stand it, I thought we could. Whatever happened, he said, we should not lose by it."[24]

Mary worried that their baby would be born while Sewall was away, but Bill was back in time for the birth, and "scarcely left the premises."[25] It was a girl, and they named her Lucretia Day Sewall, after another of Bill's aunts, though everyone called her "Kittie." The Sewalls joyously celebrated the birth of their first child and waited anxiously for word from Roosevelt about his ranch in Dakota Territory.

When TR returned to the Badlands in June 1884 to inspect his herd, he was heartened to find that, despite all the warnings of a harsh winter, the cattle had come through fine. He then took off on a hunt to try and clear his head.

Roosevelt's letter, when it finally arrived in Island Falls in July, laid it all out for Sewall in typically forthright manner:

> Now, a little plain talk, though I do not think it necessary for I know you too well. If you are afraid of hard work and privation, do not come West. If you expect to make a fortune in a year or two, do not come West. If you will give up under temporary discouragements, do not come West. If, on the other hand, you are willing to work hard, especially the first year; if you realize that for a couple of years you cannot expect to make much more than you are now making; and if you also know that at the end of that time you will be in receipt of about a thousand dollars for the third year, with an unlimited rise ahead of you and a future as bright as you yourself choose to make it—then come. Now I take for granted you will not hesitate at this time. So fix up your affairs at once, and be ready to start before the end of this month.[26]

As they'd discussed earlier in the spring, Roosevelt had drawn up a contract that basically protected Sewall and his nephew from any financial risk. So the the two Mainers had nothing to lose, potentially a lot to gain, and better still, a promised adventure with their friend.

Understandably, the letter caused a flurry of activity and emotion at the Sewall House. Bill and Wilmot talked hour upon hour about becoming cowboys, ignoring almost everything else, Mary recalled.[27] She was reminded of a previous time when Sewall's friends had lured him with descriptions of the economic opportunities in Minnesota. Now, the chance to be with his friend Theodore added to the appeal. Sewall still had to ponder the idea; it wasn't an automatic decision. Their Island Falls home was very dear to her and William, as Mary put it, but Roosevelt wrote glowingly of the beautiful, wild Badlands and the untold adventures they could encounter in the Wild West.[28]

As a new mother, Mary felt much anxiety at the prospect of making such an enormous change in their lives, but when she suggested that pioneering in a new territory peopled with Indians and outlaws might not be the best thing for baby Kittie, Bill brushed aside her worries with "a burst of enthusiasm."[29]

It took Sewall and Dow all of three days to make up their minds—they were going. They'd be in New York ready to begin the journey to Dakota Territory on July 28. Their plan was that within a year Wilmot would return to marry Lizzie Edwards, the woman he'd been courting, and then Mary and Kittie would travel with the newlyweds back to the Badlands.

Mary fumed that Bill had made the decision unilaterally and that he was up and leaving her and their newborn. After stewing for days, she vowed that she'd tell him he could not go, though she knew Bill was not one to be told what he could or couldn't do. "He had given his word," she understood, "and his determination was as great as his hero worship." When she finally summoned the courage to confront him, she stormed into the shed where he was packing tools. When she said his name and he turned to look at her, though, her resolve collapsed immediately. She could see by the look in his eyes that he felt worse than she did about their impending separation.[30]

A tense week passed as Bill and Wilmot readied their affairs. When the day arrived, several friends arrived at dawn to see the pair off, and the Sewall House was filled with laughter and tears. Bill's mother "lost the composure of which she was so proud," and his sister Sarah told him to go make his fortune and then "return and live in his real home."[31] And she assured him that she and Dave would take care of the Sewall House while he was gone.

Badlands Babies

From the outset, Bill Sewall had doubts about his new home in Dakota Territory. "It struck me that the man who first called that part of the world the 'Badlands' had hit it about right,"[1] the guide quipped. He and Dow had met Roosevelt in New York on July 28 as planned, and they reached Chimney Butte Ranch, eight miles south of Medora, on the first of August. Sewall made a quick assessment of the landscape, and, never one for pretense, he didn't hesitate to express his thoughts to his new boss.

"The first night we were at Chimney Butte," he would write later, "Roosevelt asked me what I thought of the country. I told him that I liked the country well enough but that I didn't believe that it was much of a cattle country. 'Well,' he said, 'Bill, you don't know anything about it. Everybody that's here says that it is.' I said that it was a fact that I didn't know anything about it. I realized that. But it was the way it looked to me, like not much of a cattle country."[2]

The Maine guide was on to something. As he already knew from Roosevelt's previous trips and the New Yorker's concern about the wintering cattle, the weather here was extreme. The winters were as cold as an iced-in lake and summers were hot as a campfire. Not only was it hot, but the heat brought a desiccating dryness. The man who deemed the place the Badlands, Sewall said, "found that the country was so barren and desolate that there was no game of any kind, and the weather so dry and hot that their wagons came to pieces. Their provisions ran short and they had a very hard, difficult time getting through. For that reason he named the country the 'Badlands.' I don't imagine they could have a better name."[3]

Sewall also liked the description of the lands offered up by a cavalry soldier who had passed through the country years before: he had said he "didn't know they were like anything, unless it was hell with the fire gone out." On hot summer days, as the man from Maine wryly noted, "you wouldn't exactly agree that the fire had really gone out. I recall one Fourth of July, especially, when the temperature was 125 degrees in the shade with a strong hot wind which killed almost every green thing in the country."[4]

Parched it was. The average annual rainfall was a mere fifteen inches compared to the forty-plus the Mainers were used to seeing. It was as if the hot sun just evaporated every drop before it could hit. The landscape was brown and withered, and the waterways looked like coffee with milk.[5]

The brown grass didn't seem to faze anyone in the ranching industry, however. Medora was growing like a riverside reed. The town was only slightly more bustling than Island Falls, but the feeling that something was happening—that a boom was imminent—was palpable. Many were building or talking of building, and everyone was confident that money, good money, was just waiting to be made.

The Marquis de Mores, a French nobleman, certainly thought so. He'd arrived in 1883, and, realizing that the Little Missouri River and the rail line gave him most of what he needed, he quickly became a prominent local businessman and president of the Northern Pacific Refrigerator Car Company. Dark and dashing, the marquis built the town the same way the Sewalls had built Island Falls, naming it for his wife, Medora Von Hoffman. He constructed a twenty-six-room mansion for her, the Chateau de Mores, near the river with sweeping views of the prairie and hills.

De Mores also built the area's slaughterhouse—the big beef-processing plant— on the other side of the water. Thus he held the keys to the local cattle industry. When it opened, the meat-packing plant inspired quite a commotion among other businessmen. By 1884, the dusty town had a population of 250, a brickyard, several stores, a newspaper, a hotel, a Catholic church, and the requisite saloon.[6]

In that saloon you could count on finding a certain type of personality. There was still a lot of the Wild West to Medora when Roosevelt arrived—giving another meaning to the term *Badlands*—and the shadier characters seemed drawn into the employ of de Mores. "He didn't give [them] active encouragement," remembered W.T. Dantz, a neighbor of Roosevelt's, "but his money attracted them and [they] clustered around the Marquis camp."[7] Sewall and Dow and TR would get to know these men over gun barrels.

Roosevelt may have been disappointed with Sewall's initial reaction to the Badlands, but he didn't seem to dwell on it. Quite the contrary. He wrote his sister Bamie, "Everything so far has gone along beautifully. I had great fun bringing my two backwoods babies out here. Their absolute astonishment and delight at everything they saw, and their really very shrewd, and yet wonderfully simple remarks were a perfect delight to me."

Undaunted, the Mainers jumped right in. Or rather right on. Roosevelt gave Sewall and Dow each a pony, paired them with an old sea captain named Robins who was working for him, and set them off with a hundred head of cattle to push the thirty-five miles down the river to the site of TR's new ranch.

Curiously, this was Sewall's first time on horseback—in Maine, folks didn't as much ride horses as use them to pull things—and TR found it a hoot. He wrote Bamie, "They looked the picture of dreary discomfort, Sewall remarking that his only previous experience in the equestrian line was when he 'rode logs.'"[8]

The guide "got along riding all right," he would tell his brother later, but he didn't care for Robins, who kept trying to hurry him along. "He was a man of many orders," Sewall recalled. "I was green of course and had a green pony. . . . He rode up to me with great vehemence of word and manner to hurry me up. Said if I did not help him more he should kill his horse. I told him in about the shortest manner I could that I did not care anything about his horse or him. That I was doing as well as I could and wasn't going to be found fault with. He evidently did not think me a pleasant companion and left me; after that we got along fine."[9]

The former sea captain went straight to Dow. "That Sewall is a kind of quick-tempered fellow," he said.

"I don't think he is," Dow replied.

"He snapped me up," said Robins.

"You must have said something to him," said Dow, "for he ain't in the habit of doing such things."[10]

Sewall did what he could to keep up with the party, but he and his steed disagreed. When he tried to spur the beast on, it promptly deposited him in a washout. The laconic Island Falls man could see the humor in the situation, though, writing to his brother about the pony, "[W]e have had a number of differences and controversies, but my arguments have always prevailed so far." Before too long, Sewall had given his mount a name: "I have named him Fallback because he always falls back behind unless he is obliged to keep up."[11]

Driving cattle was also a new experience for Sewall. The Maine guide, so experienced in the outdoors, found himself in a whole new world. The cowboys pushed the young short-horns toward the ranch by day, and at night took turns riding around the stationary herd to make sure none of the big beasts strayed, moving quietly so as not to provoke a stampede. Despite their early differences, Sewall and Dow apparently impressed the bossy sea captain. "You've got two good men here," Robins told Roosevelt. "That Sewall don't calculate to bear anything. I spoke to him the other day, and he snapped me up so short I did not know what to make of it. But I don't blame him, I did not speak to him as I ought."[12]

In the thirty-five miles between Medora and the ranch site, the trail crossed the Little Missouri twenty-two times by Sewall's calculation. When they drew closer to the spot TR had selected for Elkhorn, in a valley between high bluffs along the river, they found a hardscrabble old hunting shack. The derelict cabin was on land granted to the Northern Pacific Railroad Company by the federal government but somehow Roosevelt had been able to take over the squatter's rights to the property from its previous occupant for $400. The nearest ranch was about ten miles to the south, another was a couple miles farther north toward Medora.

Sewall found the surrounding landscape "strange and interesting," and he thought the way the water had carved up the hills in the distance gave them the look of ruined castles. "We built the house in a clump of large cottonwood trees near the bank of the Little Missouri river," he wrote, describing the lay of the land. "West from the house it was smooth and grassy for about a hundred yards, then there was a belt of cottonwoods which went back for some two hundred yards. They were the largest trees I ever saw in Dakota and it was from them that we got most of the timber for the house. Back of them the steep clay hills rose to the height of two or three hundred feet and looked like miniature mountains. A little to the northwest was a hill with coal veins in it which burned red in the dark. To the east we looked across the river about two hundred yards, then across a wide bottom covered with grass, sage-brush, and some small trees to the steep clay hills which rose almost perpendicular from the river bottom. Beyond that was the Badlands for perhaps twenty miles."[13]

Even though he found the site intriguing, the guide's misgivings about Dakota Territory continued. In a letter to his brother Sam, he called the river—"meanest apology for a frog pond I ever saw"—and its environs "a queer country." Within a month of moving in, he wrote again to Sam, saying, "You would like to see it but you would not want to live here long."[14]

Once at their destination, Sewall and Dow knew what they had to do. They couldn't be ranchers without a proper ranch. And, of course, felling trees, peeling logs, and constructing buildings was something they were infinitely better at than playing cowboy. Their prowess with axes drew the admiration of their neighbors, who found them curiosities. (They called Bill the "Old Mennonite," probably because he didn't drink, smoke, or swear.[15]) One neighbor, John Goodall, said the pair were "good in hewing logs but were a nuisance around livestock."[16]

They spent a few months preparing the site, working from early October to New Year's, and being nuisances around the livestock. "It was new work to Dow and myself, and we liked it," Sewall said. "It was interesting. Besides, the wild, desolate grandeur of the country had a kind of charm."[17]

Exceptional cowboys or not, Sewall and Dow didn't have any trouble babysitting cattle. They were busy watching the herd until the end of August. "It's not hard work to look after them,"[18] Bill would write his brother. Roosevelt took his two Maine friends south on their first roundup, collecting cattle seared with Roosevelt's Maltese Cross and Triangle brands. They followed the Fort Keogh Trail for weeks to the foot of the Big Horn Mountains in central Wyoming.

About this time Roosevelt tried to coax Sewall into his first Western hunting trip. "While we were cutting the timber Theodore went to the Big Horn Mountains for an elk hunt. He wanted me to go with him, but I disliked to leave Dow alone, knowing, if I went, one man would not be much of a crew to work on the house; so I prevailed on Roosevelt to get a man who was familiar with the country to go with him. I never wanted to go on a hunt so much as that one."[19] TR cheerfully returned days later with not only a bull elk but also a grizzly to show for his travels.

As the men from Maine felled cottonwoods to be used for their log house, Roosevelt eagerly helped out, but while he had more experience in some of the ways of the rancher—riding, cattle pushing—he was outmatched when it came to the use of an ax. One night, after a day of felling, TR to his amusement overheard one of the local hands ask Dow how the cutting was going. "Well, Bill cut down fifty-three," Wilmot reported, "I cut forty-nine, and the boss, the boss he beavered down seventeen."[20]

Medora's most prominent resident didn't care much for Roosevelt's new enterprise. "De Mores had about the toughest lot of cowboys in that part of the country, and there was trouble continually,"[21] Sewall recalled. The Marquis de Mores took exception to the site his young New York neighbor had chosen for his ranch and sent Roosevelt a note saying that he was building on land de Mores claimed as his own.

The vast open space here was largely owned by the Northern Pacific Railroad or the federal government, and squatting was a long-established tradition. Roosevelt responded that he had found only dead sheep on the property and he didn't figure they would mind his being out there. He heard nothing back, but when he needed to return to Chimney Butte Ranch, he warned Sewall and Dow to be on the lookout for trouble. "I cal'late we can look out for ourselves,"[22] Sewall assured him.

The fact that no one really owned any of this land was something that bothered the Mainer. In a letter to his brother, he likened it to driving logs across Mattawamkeag Lake when one team's timbers get mixed with the next: "About the only way is to stand your hand right or wrong," he wrote. "I don't like it and never did. I want to control and manage my own affairs and have a right to what I do have. But here as on the lake it is common [property,] and one has as much right as another."[23]

The marquis was insistent about *his* presumed rights, though, and he and his men continued to press the newcomers. One Sunday morning, Will Dow was out for a walk and Sewall was writing a letter when suddenly they both heard gunfire—"a great fusillade; something over twenty guns were fired as fast as I could count," according to Sewall. Within minutes, a half dozen cowboys pulled up at the shack. "I knew one of them as the right-hand man of the Marquis de Mores, and decided that they had come down to look us over."[24]

Sizing up the situation, Sewall chose to confront the gang with some hospitality and asked them in. Lunchtime was approaching, and the Maine men had prepared a good pot of beanhole beans. "I made them some coffee," Sewall explained, "and got out all the best things we had in the shack. I had decided to treat them just as nicely as I knew how." He kept his eye on their leader for any sign that more trouble was about to materialize. "I think he had had a little whiskey, as he certainly had a very sharp appetite."

But nothing untoward happened. The gang's ringleader was disarmed by the unexpected hospitality. "He said he never saw such good baked beans and he didn't know when he had had anything as good as they were. I had plenty of beans and kept urging him to have more. I knew that that was a good way to make a man feel good-natured."

After they ate they all stepped outside and looked the site over. "They thought we had a very nice place, fixed up very nice, and didn't find any fault with anything," Sewall continued. "The party rode off and I didn't hear any more shooting. . . . I was always treated very nicely by that man afterward and he seemed very friendly." This was a good thing, as the man had a reputation for drawing blood. "He had killed one man they were sure of and they thought he had killed another."

The marquis himself was hardly satisfied, however, nor were all of his other lieutenants. On another occasion one of de Mores's henchmen came by and told Sewall and Dow he intended to shoot their boss. "I told Theodore about it when he came back," Sewall said later. "He said, 'Is that so?'"[25] Roosevelt saddled his horse and rode straight to where that particular cowboy lived and demanded to know who was threatening him and why. "The man was flabbergasted, I guess, by Roosevelt's directness," according to Sewall, and claimed he had been misquoted. Again, the affair ended well, and the man and TR were even friendly afterward.

Bill Sewall was forever impressed by the gumption Roosevelt showed in such situations, describing him as "afraid of nothing and nobody." He liked to tell the story of a time when TR was in a small saloon and was confronted by a "bad man" who didn't like the look of him. This outlaw had been drinking, and he'd heard about the newcomer with the spectacles who thought he could operate a ranch. "Theodore was not a big man—he was only medium height weighing about a hundred and fifty pounds, and he wore glasses. But grit to the heel! The fellow called him a 'four-eyed tenderfoot' and tried to take his measure in abusive language." Roosevelt ignored him, and the thug "naturally concluded that he was afraid of him." Not so, as the man would discover in the next instant. "Suddenly, Roosevelt let out and caught him on the butt of the jaw—and he flattened out. This gained him some reputation."[26]

There were enough of these sorts of encounters, though, that Sewall and Dow always remained vigilant. Later in the fall of 1884, while Roosevelt was away on another trip, they heard that the same man who had threatened Roosevelt was now threatening them. "Dow happened to overhear two men talking about us," Sewall would later write. "They were not unfriendly to us, but they had evidently heard the threats. One remarked to the other there would be dead men around that old shack where we were, some day."

The Aroostook men decided that "if there were any dead men there, it would not be us." They went about their work as usual, but were always watchful and kept their guns handy, "where we could pick them up in an instant," Sewall explained. "We were working at the edge of a piece of timber and there was quite a thicket behind us. We knew that if anybody came, he would come by the trail and we intended to make for the timber, and if he wanted to hunt us there, why, we would see who was best at the business."[27]

Despite such distractions, they made steady progress on the ranch house. Elkhorn was to measure sixty feet by thirty feet with a veranda out front—Sewall and Dow called it a porch, of course—and eight or ten rooms, depending upon whose account you believe. Theodore Roosevelt, Bill Sewall, and Roosevelt's future wife, Edith Carow, who would pay a visit, all described it differently. Sewall took credit for its architecture—"I designed the house myself," he wrote, "and it was a sizable place"[28]—but drawings by the boss suggest it was he who came up with the basic outline of the place.

While the Elkhorn house was being built, TR spent most of his time at Chimney Butte when he was in the Badlands. He seemed in no particular hurry to get Elkhorn finished. He thought it was just as important that his men got a chance to hunt and explore their new home, and he instructed them to take at least one day off every week to get out. Since another full day was usually eaten up by a weekly trip to Medora for mail and supplies, that left a five-day work week, which Sewall considered "half time."[29]

Sewall and Dow cut timber until it became too cold to keep working. "I remember the morning that we began to put up the walls the thermometer was sixty-five degrees below zero," Sewall wrote. "This was the coldest weather I have ever experienced. No one suffered much from the heat the next three weeks. The thermometer ranged from thirty to sixty-five below most of the time."[30] Their thermometer would eventually break from the cold, and the two friends would endure that frigid winter in a "dugout tunneled into the bank of the river."[31]

During the days of Roosevelt-encouraged exploration, Sewall confirmed his earlier suspicions—the Badlands weren't for him. During his first month there, in 1884, he wrote Sam again to assure him that he had no reason to be envious: "The people live better there than here and it is a better country to live than any I have seen, and if I make money here just as soon as I get enough to live on you will see me back—the quicker the better."[32]

By winter he was even more insistent. One cold February day he wrote to the family back in Island Falls: "My grit is good but I believe it is better country to live in at home than here and if I don't change my mind—*very much*—shall return as soon as possible."[33]

The list of things he didn't like about his new home grew daily. The extreme weather was one complaint. In February it was bitter cold, but in summer it was "hot enough to make a rattlesnake pant."[34] The people were listless: "[I]t's not the plan to work very hard here," he wrote, "the workers are a lazy set."[35] It was barren and desolate and a good place for wildlife to die. "I think the country ought to have been left to the animals that have laid bones here."[36] And he missed the sweeter things. "It makes me pretty fierce to think of the berries and fish but I can stand it as I have I suppose."[37]

And after spending time on the range, Sewall still wasn't convinced the Badlands were meant for cattle. "Don't say anything about what I am writing out of the family," he instructed his brother, "but the stock business is a new business here in the Badlands and I can't find as anybody has made anything at it yet. They all *expect to*. I think all have lost as yet."[38]

TR had concerns of his own. The events of the previous February were still fixed in his mind, much as he tried to escape them. He was "very melancholy at times," remembered Sewall. "He told me one day that he felt as if it did not make any difference what became of him—he had nothing to live for. . . . I used to go for him bow-legged when he talked like that." Sewall tried to impress upon his friend all the good he had in his life, and the future that he had ahead of him. And he had a more important concern. "You have your child to live for," Sewall told him.

"Her aunt can take care of her a good deal better than I can," Roosevelt responded. "She would be just as well off without me."

This earned TR a full-on Bill Sewall lecture, and again the guide seemed to have a keen prescience. "You won't always feel as you do now," he told the urban cowboy, "and you won't always be willing to stay here and drive cattle, because when you get to feeling differently you will want to get back among your friends and associates where you can do more and be more benefit to the world than you can here driving cattle. If you cannot think of anything else to do you can go home and start a reform. You would make a good reformer. You always want to make things better instead of worse."[39]

When he could get out of his funk, though, Roosevelt was far more content with the life of a ranchman than were either of the two Mainers, so much so that he wasn't sure he ever wanted to leave it. He wrote his good friend Henry Cabot Lodge on November 23, "my cattle are looking well—and in fact the statesman of the past has merged, alas, I fear, forever into the cowboy of the present."[40]

Roosevelt's sister Corinne could see this actually happening to her brother. "All his craving for the out-of-door life," she wrote, "all his sympathy with pioneer enterprise, such as his heroes Davy Crockett and Daniel Boone had indulged in, were satisfied by those long days on the open prairies, and by the building of his ranch-houses, with the assistance of his old friends Bill Sewall and Will Dow."[41]

Cowpunching

Most of the time Bill Sewall found himself too busy to dwell on his doubts about the Badlands. When it grew too cold for construction, he and Dow and a couple of their neighbors ventured sixty miles downriver to visit a village of the Gros Ventre tribe, Montana Indians who were related to the Arapaho. They'd met an Indian trader named James Watts who had made a real impression on Sewall—"he is a genuine specimen of a frontier man," Bill wrote his brother, "just like you have read of and seen pictures of."[1] Watts seemed to like the Mainers, too, and invited them to his lodge in the Gros Ventre community.

Sewall was captivated by the reservation, too, and bought moccasins, buckskins, buffalo robes, war plumes, and a mountain lion skin. He saw little, three-inch Sioux and Mandan scalps for sale for five dollars, but thought they were too expensive. "It would be cheaper to take one myself if I wanted it badly," he joked. He and Dow were asked to join the village in a feast and a Native council where the peace pipe was offered to them. Ever the antismoker, Sewall declined—"Will took a wiff. I passed."

The Natives found the big, bearded Mainer as much a curiosity as he found them, and one man actually began to braid his whiskers, which Sewall patiently endured until the guy picked up a big blade, as if to cut them off. "I had been watching him closely," he said, "and when he reached for the knife I grabbed him by the top of the head quick and motioned as if I was going to strike. I think it really scared him and they all laughed."[2]

This was but one of the many long journeys Sewall made in the saddle. He and Dow traveled frequently to Medora, hunted in the nearby area, and participated in a handful of roundups, which meant days on horseback.

The most extensive of these roundups came in the summer of 1885, just after Dow had returned home to marry Lizzie, and TR had gone to New York. Sewall saddled up as part of a posse searching for lost and stolen cattle and horses, traveling five hundred miles over eighteen days, through "as wild and unsettled portion of the country as can be found now, so the people here say," he wrote.

The trip took the guide and six companions through a large chunk of the West—from Montana to the Big Bend country in southwest Texas, a region known to harbor horse thieves, cutthroats, and various Indian tribes. "The oldest heads seemed to think there might be some danger,"[3] Sewall reported, but the men were prepared to handle whatever they came across, each carrying six-shooting Frontier revolvers. Two had Winchester repeating rifles.

None of the threats materialized. As Sewall noted in another letter to his brother, brigands, highwaymen, and horse thieves typically avoided ranchers, who were usually well armed and who understood the horse thieves' ways and often could outfox them. The Elkhorn party did encounter a band of Gros Ventre Indians, but they were friendly enough.

The Maine man was fascinated by much of what he saw—a dead Indian in a tent, a two-hour hailstorm, graves of dead cavalry soldiers, acres of wild roses. And he greatly appreciated the opportunity to spend time in this company, which included men from Florida, Texas, and Kentucky—all old, experienced cattlemen except himself and one other. "I found the cowboys to be good companions," he wrote, "the same class of men I was used to being with at home, only they were engaged in a different business. They were pleasant, kind-hearted men who were all right unless they had whiskey, and were no worse than our men of the same class under the same conditions."[4]

Nonetheless, he returned to the ranch more convinced than ever that his home was in the East. "I don't like such a country and don't think you would," he wrote to his brother Sam. "It is very pretty to look at but I soon get tired of it. There is too much of one thing and no good water. . . . I would not live all my life here for the whole Territory, but I had a good time and enjoyed the trip for I got a better idea of the country and the people that live in it than I have had before."[5]

These misgivings make it hard to fathom why Sewall—and Dow with him—signed a new contract with Roosevelt in June of 1885. The guide's commitment to duty and loyalty must have trumped his dislike of Dakota. The agreement read as follows:

Little Missouri, Dakota

We the undersigned, Theodore Roosevelt, party of the first part, and William Sewall and Wilmot S. Dow, parties of the second part, do agree and contract as follows.

1. The party of the first part having put eleven hundred head of cattle, valued at twenty-five thousand dollars ($25,000) on the Elkhorn Ranche, on the little Missouri river, the parties of the

second part do agree to take charge of said cattle for the space of three years, and at the end of this time agree to return to said party of the first part the equivalent in value of the original herd (twenty-five thousand dollars); any increase in value of the herd over said sum of twenty-five thousand dollars is to belong two-thirds to said party of the first part and one-third to said parties of the second part.

2. From time to time said parties of the second part shall in the exercise of their best judgment make sales of such cattle as are fit for market, the moneys obtained by said sales to be two-thirds to said party of the first part and one third to said parties of the second part; but no sales of cattle shall be made sufficient in amount to reduce the herd below its original value save by the direction in writing of the party of the first part.

3. The parties of the second part are to keep accurate accounts of expenditures, losses, the calf crop, etc.; said accounts to always be open to the inspection of the party of the first part.

4. The parties of the second part are to take good care of the cattle, and also of the ponies, buildings, etc., belonging to said party of the first part.

Signed,
THEODORE ROOSEVELT (party of the first part)
W.W. SEWALL
W.S. DOW
(parties of the second part).[6]

Shortly after the long round-up, Sewall drove to Medora to pick up Dow and his new wife, Lizzie, his own wife, Mary, and their daughter, Kittie. After a year apart, both were excited to be reunited. Mary thought her husband the cowboy looked "leaner, much tanned, and his face was intensely alive," and she enjoyed the ride to the ranch, Kittie sitting in Bill's lap. When they reached their corner of the Little Missouri, the sun was silhouetting the distant buttes, and Bill pointed out Elkhorn proudly. "What a pretty sight!" Mary exclaimed.

Bill readied dinner, announcing that while he was pleased to be resigning his position as cook, he would prepare one last meal of biscuits and steak just to show the ladies that he could cook western style.[7] The arrival of family temporarily made Sewall a little more comfortable. "You may suppose I was not sorry to see them," he wrote his brother. "They like it better than they expected to."[8]

The Sewalls and Dows settled into a routine. Bill and Wilmot worked on building stables, sheds, and outbuildings when the weather was cooperative. In the summer Bill also gardened, planting peas and squash and potatoes. When the conditions were not right for construction, because of rain or cold, the two frequently rode into the surrounding woods and meadows to take deer. And every few months the pair would get roped into another roundup.

Mary and Lizzie got along fine and made the transition to ranch life easily enough. They were both used to rural living and put in hours cleaning, sewing, and cooking, sometimes preparing meals for as many as twenty hands during a roundup. They even straightened Mr. Roosevelt's things on occasion. But the two wives found homesteading along the Little Missouri a far cry from village life in Aroostook County. Bill's vegetable gardens withered in the summer heat, and the water was so alkaline that it made Kittie sick. They had to buy lemons by the crate to make it potable. Perhaps because there were far fewer people, Mary found her work less demanding here than at the Sewall House, and in her free time she enjoyed TR's books, the rocker on the porch, and especially horseback riding. Roosevelt bought the women sidesaddles ("one $28 and the other cost $35") and they both were fond of a little gray horse named Ted.[9]

Mary always felt a little uncomfortable, though, that Elkhorn wasn't their home but Roosevelt's. She liked TR, and he tried to reassure her —"I hope you'll feel that this is your true home and do things your way"—but the fact that they were effectively tenants nagged at Mary. "Mr. Roosevelt's plans, preferences and orders would prevail."[10]

The neighbors found the idea of two women in the same household amusing, and they used to tease the Sewalls that "no house is big enough to hold two women,"[11] as Bill would recall. "But there was never any harsh word spoken at Elkhorn ranch," he reported, "and I have an idea that those were the most peaceful years of Roosevelt's life. He spent most of the time with us[,] going east very little. He loved the desolate country, as we all did. . . . He worked like the rest of us and occasionally he worked longer than any of the rest of us, for often when we were through with the day's work he would go to his room and write. . . . more often, however, he would sit before the fire cold autumn or winter nights and tell stories of his hunting trips or about history that he had read. He was the best-read man I ever saw or ever heard of, and he seemed to remember everything he read."[12]

This was Mary's impression as well. Roosevelt was unlike any other man in her experience. Bill read, but not anywhere near the extent that TR did. The New Yorker also wrote "hour after hour." He received and sent voluminous quantities of mail and seemed to have more than just one foot back in his home state—more like a leg. From hearing his conversations with her husband, Mary knew that Roosevelt kept a keen eye on both New York and national politics.[13]

Roosevelt seemed to enjoy the arrival of the Sewall family, but his routine was rattled a bit by their littlest member. There was a certain annoyance in the tone of a letter he wrote to Bamie in New York, asking her to please send some toys for the child. Kittie didn't have any—or any playmates—and thus was constantly demanding attention. "The poor little mite of a Sewall girl, just baby Lee's age, has neither playmates nor play toys. I don't appreciate it as a table companion, especially when fed on, or rather feeding itself on, a mixture of syrup and strawberry jam (giving it the look of a dirty little yellow haired gnome in war paint)."[14] He also asked Bamie to send a picture of baby Alice to Bill's mother in Island Falls, because he was fond of her and knew she would enjoy it.

Roosevelt considered the porch and its rockers, his books, and the open fireplace his "special luxuries," but he was happy to share. "I think Mrs. Sewall and Mrs. Dow enjoyed them almost as much as I did."[15]

The women didn't leave Elkhorn much, but relished the opportunity to travel into town, to go riding, or to pay a social call. Five miles from the nearest neighbor, their remote ranch was more like an island than *Island* Falls was. Because of the physical isolation of Elkhorn—and the closeness she felt to everyone back in "The Falls"—Mary began to feel very cut off from the world. They all felt a void in their lives. Living on a ranch thirty-five miles from Medora, they dearly missed the constant comings and goings of their hometown and hungered for news from there, bad as well as good, and concerning other families as well as their own.[16] This was never more acute than in winter, when they barely got outside the house at all. Bill and Wilmot at least went to Medora occasionally.

Mary tried to convince herself that she was content. In March of 1886 she wrote her sister, "we will be glad when the time comes for us to start back home, not because we are homesick for we are not." But she was, and eventually she would lament to friends back home that there were few opportunities to leave the confines of the ranch—no Sunday school, no meetings, "or anyplace we can go when we get tired of staying in the house."[17] Within a couple of months she was more forthright, stating frankly to her sister Annie, "I have been some lonesome."[18]

Her husband, of course, wasn't any happier. By December of 1885, he had another chance to see how the animals would handle the weather. He didn't think Elkhorn would lose many head, but he didn't like the odds for the "she cattle," which were weakened from calving: "[T]he calves suck them down and they don't get any chance to gain up before they have another calf, and then if the weather is very cold they are pretty sure to die." He was also leery of the influx of large herds into the territory: "They are crowding in cattle all the time and I think they will eat us out in a few years."[19]

There were hints that Roosevelt had his own reservations about their venture. He, too, worried about how the herd would fare during the impending cold season: "I hope the cattle will come through this winter well. Keep as sharp an eye on them as possible, both for the weak ones and to see if there are any great number straying off. . . . I have so much money invested in the cattle business that I must make it come out well or I will be hauled up pretty short."[20]

Theodore Roosevelt was building more than just a ranch in the Badlands. When he wasn't busy at Elkhorn, he could often be found in Medora, helping to put together a cattlemen's association, naturally gravitating toward the politics of the community. The new organization was to a certain extent intended to settle disputes—such as the ones his crew had with de Mores—but more specifically it was "to protect their interests against unjust interference from the outside,"[21] as he said in a notice advertising a meeting that was posted all over town. He took to organizing with his typical vigor.

Roosevelt's leadership abilities and genuine enthusiasm soon endeared him to his neighbors, and he became the chairman of the Little Missouri Stockman's Association. One of the Ferris brothers' friends, Jack Reuter, recalled his initial impression of TR: "The first time I met him was in 1883 when he bought some cattle off Wadsworth and Hawley. He struck me like a sort of rough and ready, all-around frontiersman. Wasn't a bit stuck up, just the same as one of the rest of us."[22]

The new chairman used his position to upbraid some of the characters in town who he thought had it coming. When the association had convened its first meeting in Medora, in 1884, Roosevelt took the floor. Among the crowd were a deputy U.S. marshal who was suspected of being corrupt and a few of de Mores' cronies, and Roosevelt directed his remarks right at them. As historian Hermann Hagedorn put it, with a certain amount of hyperbole: "People called this the beginning of law and order in the Wild West."[23]

But TR still had to deal with the marquis. The Frenchman continued to make known his displeasure with Roosevelt and his outfit. In the spring of 1885, he sent the New Yorker a letter that, as Sewall put it, "nearly resulted in a duel."

"Roosevelt read me the letter and said that he regarded it as a threat that the Marquis would, perhaps, challenge him," the guide recalled. "If he did, he should accept the challenge, for he would not be bullied. . . . he told me that if he was challenged, he wanted me to act as his second."

This wasn't part of the land-rights argument that de Mores had been concerned about in the past. This time the marquis had been implicated in the murder of a man he accused of squatting, and one of the men who worked for neighboring rancher Joe Ferris was summoned to testify against him. Apparently de Mores thought Roosevelt had put up the witness's travel expenses and "furnished money for the prosecution." His letter allowed as much and closed with the statement that there was "always a way to settle such difficulties between gentlemen."

Roosevelt threw it right back at de Mores, insisting that he harbored no grudge toward him and had not provided any assistance to anyone. But, as Sewall recalled, "as the closing sentence of the Marquis's letter implied a threat, he felt it a duty to himself to say that at all times and in all places he was ready to answer for his actions." Sewall told TR he thought that instead of a date for a duel he'd get an apology. Roosevelt figured the marquis might choose to ignore the letter, but he didn't think the man would apologize.

A few days afterward, the boss strolled up to Sewall with a letter in his hands and told him he was right. This time de Mores had written that there was "always a way to settle misunderstandings between gentlemen—without trouble"—and invited Roosevelt to dinner.[24]

The West didn't get any wilder for Sewall and Roosevelt than in the spring of 1886. Roosevelt had just returned from back east when the area was hit by a big storm—a "snorter," in the guide's estimation.[25] Bill went out to check on the skiff they kept beside the river, a fancy little craft that Roosevelt had bought in St. Paul and that Sewall called "the best one on the river."[26] The little boat was gone—none too surprising considering the recent weather conditions. But when he looked closer, Sewall found that it wasn't the gale that had taken the boat downstream—the line had been cut. Dow spied a mitten nearby on the ground that none of them could account for and surmised it had probably been dropped by the thief or thieves.

Roosevelt wanted to take off after the culprits right then and there, but they didn't have another boat, and Sewall reminded him he wouldn't get far with the ice and alders. He explained to TR that he could make a boat, it would just take a little time.

Four days, in fact. When Sewall's homemade vessel was ready, Roosevelt was as eager as the spring freshet, but cold and ice floes kept them at the ranch for several more days. Finally it was safe enough to go, and the three men piled in. The worries of both wives followed them downstream. Because of the lawlessness of the land Mary admitted she was anxious whenever any of the men left Elkhorn. "There was talk at the ranch of unfriendly ranchers and out-laws," as well as "harsh terrain" and "frequent, violent thunderstorms."[27]

It was apparently a less troubling prospect for the little posse. Even a chase after bandits couldn't make Theodore Roosevelt, Bill Sewall, and Wilmot Dow pass up a good opportunity to hunt, and they bagged two deer as they traveled along the river. To fill idle moments Roosevelt brought a book along, making his way through *Anna Karenina*. They spent their first night camped on the riverbank, and the next day they rounded a bend in the river and spotted TR's boat.

Sewall pulled their craft ashore and hitched it, and told the other two to get their pistols ready. Even though he was the "boss," Roosevelt would still seek Sewall's counsel and even defer to him. "I was the oldest man in the party, and the two younger men looked to me for advice and were always ready to do as I said, thinking that it was probably best," Sewall recalled. "I felt a good deal of responsibility."[28]

The guide encouraged caution. "It was rather funny business for one of the men was called a pretty hard ticket [and we knew he] was armed with a Winchester rifle and a self-cocking Smith and Wesson revolver which are considered the most dangerous kind of pistol,"[29] Sewall explained in an account of the episode he later sent to his brother.

The "hard ticket" he was referring to was Mike "Red" Finnegan, who indeed had a reputation as a "shooter." Legend had it that one afternoon he had gone on a rampage and shot up Medora, putting holes in the offices of the *Badlands Cowboy* and the local oyster house and sending the whole population into hiding.[30] As Bill Dantz, Roosevelt's Little Missouri neighbor, described it: "He laid down in a fringe of bush near the Marquis's store where he could command a clear view of the town and began to pump lead into everything in sight."[31] Sewall didn't want to be on the receiving end of one of Finnegan's volleys: "If he was in the bushes and saw us first he was liable to make it very unhealthy for us."[32]

Luckily, Finnegan wasn't in the bushes. The three men were able to march into camp and corral the one member of the thieving party who was there, an older German fellow who put up no resistance. But his two colleagues were not to be found. The man was named Chris, and, as Sewall described him later, "he was really a tool of the king thieves, Finnegan and Bernstadt, two of the worst pirates in the Badlands."[33]

The camp was located on a fifteen-foot-wide bank of the river. Behind it was another bank that rose six feet and was backed by thick bushes. Will took a position in the bushes to the right, Sewall to the left, and Roosevelt in the center, and it was TR's job to jump up and order the thieves to put their hands up when they returned. "Will and I both with double-barrel guns loaded with buck shot and we were all three going to shoot if they offered to raise a gun. It is rather savage work but it don't do to fool with such fellows. If there was killing to be done we meant to do it ourselves."[34]

They waited like this for half an hour before they heard someone coming. He was a ways off, so they had time to get ready. When the man stepped into the open TR yelled at him and he raised his hands up "very quick." The trio of lawmen "took his gun and gave him a seat under the bank with the cheerful information that if he made any noise or tried to get away we would shoot him."[35]

Their second captive wasn't the notorious Red Finnegan either. Another half hour passed, during which time Will found Finnegan's pistol, which meant he had only his rifle with him. Then the outlaw himself sauntered into camp without a hint of suspicion. Roosevelt stood up, leveled his gun, and instructed Finnegan to drop his weapon and put his hands up. When he hesitated an instant, Wilmot sprang up and snapped, "Damn you! Drop that gun!" The gunman complied, according to Sewall, but he seemed more angry than afraid. "Roosevelt warned the men that if they kept quiet and did not try to escape they would be all right but if they tried anything, we would shoot them."[36]

The thieves' camp was days away from any place with a jail, and the icy conditions on the river made travel a chore, so the three men from Elkhorn settled in themselves. Sewall, Dow, and Roosevelt took turns watching the troublemakers while the others slept. The next day Roosevelt and Dow even went off hunting, leaving their captives in the charge of the big Maine guide. "The men were none of them very formidable men physically," Sewall recalled. "I calculated I could handle the whole concern when they were unarmed." TR saw to it that the men were well treated, even if he didn't like them or their type. "We used and fed them as if they were guests but minded to keep a very sharp watch over them and gave them no chance to escape."[37] For a bunch of crooks, they were fairly well behaved.

When the ice relented after a few days and the posse was able to navigate close to the town of Dickinson, thirty-five miles east of Medora, Roosevelt took the men to stand before a justice and to be delivered to jail. The old German was released and the other two were put behind bars in Mandan, near Bismarck.

Delivering the bandits—and the evidence—took the trio three hundred miles from home, and after TR left to bring the men in, Sewall and Dow hunted their way home, bagging beaver, geese, and ducks. When TR reached Mandan, giving the sheriff the guns and stolen items the thieves had in their possession, Sewall and Dow took the train back to Medora. The entire adventure took them three weeks. Mary and Lizzie had fretted constantly while the men were away. "It had been quite an anxious time for our wives," Sewall said. And not just for the women. An older man who lived nearby had visited Elkhorn almost daily to inquire about the men. "While he had tried to make it appear that there was nothing unusual about his calls, our wives knew he was worried."[38]

The Finnegan episode was one of the longest journeys Sewall and Roosevelt would take together. "I had one of the best chances to know the real Theodore Roosevelt on this expedition," Sewall would recall. "As the Indians say, 'We ate out of the same dish and slept under the same blanket.'"[39]

In this still relatively lawless land, news of the episode traveled fast, and from Mandan to Medora people were talking about Theodore Roosevelt and his Maine men. "Think we have all got our names pretty well up by this scrape. I don't think we will have anything more stolen from us," concluded Sewall as he set the story down for his brother in page after page until his hand grew tired. He suggested to Sam that he gather people together to read it all at once. "It is the longest letter I ever wrote and I guess the longest I ever shall write and probably nobody will ever want me to write another like it."[40]

The Beef

One mercilessly hot day in August of 1886, as Sewall and Dow were hard at work, they were called into the house. Mary was in labor, and it was not going well. She was barely conscious, had lost a lot of blood, and the baby was not emerging. The nearest doctor was 110 miles away, and the midwife who was overseeing the birth was beginning to panic. Sewall, seeing that the woman was no longer able to help, sent her home. Wilmot Dow, who had delivered many cattle, sheep, and horses, rolled up his sleeves. Somehow, he was able to extract the child—little Fred—and save Mary.

It was a joyous day, but Mary remained in frail health for weeks afterward. Fred, too, was weak, and it would be more than two months before the infant would be able to lift his head. His father wrote home to Island Falls that the boy, "came like the Irishman's Elephant but did not strike hard enough to knock his brains out and we hope he has shifted ends. He seems well and all right."[1] Though she would pull through fine, it was times like this when Mary most missed Island Falls, especially her sisters, Annie and Suze, and Bill's sister Sarah.

The stork arrived again at Elkhorn the following week, when Wilmot's wife, Lizzie, added yet another resident to the ranch—Wilmot Sewall Dow, Jr. This baby's birth was much less traumatic, and he and Fred would for the rest of their lives be known—by the cowboys who came to inspect them and by the folks back in Island Falls—as the Badlands babies.

Roosevelt had been back East when these two boys were born, arriving at the ranch three days after young Wilmot did. He found Bill Sewall creating a ruckus hammering away on a cradle. When he suggested the racket was too much for the sensitive ears of the newborns, Sewall turned to him and opined that "the noise would be good for them." This tickled TR. "He laughed about that and told that story as long as he lived."[2]

When Mary was once again fit to run the household, she began hearing talk that disturbed her—the ranch was taking sizable financial losses, and Bill, Wilmot, and Theodore were all very concerned. This was the first time any of these men had faced a real failure, and they all badly wanted to reverse the trend, but to Mary, it seemed inevitable that TR would close his ranch and return to New York. The ranch had provided him an escape from his grief after losing his wife and mother, but now that he was feeling markedly better, she thought it was no surprise that he would want to return to the city, no matter how much he loved the rugged ranch life.[3]

She was fairly certain that the money woes would mean the end of their Dakota adventure, and she fervently hoped that her husband would want to return east rather than pursue other opportunities farther west. Ranching might be fine for Dakotans, she felt, but Maine was where the Sewalls and Dows belonged.[4]

Her husband, of course, felt the same way. And so did Will Dow. More circumspect than his uncle, he, too, had been quietly questioning their cowboy future. When he had returned to Island Falls to pick up his wife, he seemed to drink it all in—"the village life, the green woods and meadows, everywhere . . . a contrast to North Dakota." And while he was proud of the ranch and eager for Lizzie to see it, he privately confided to Mary that he "wondered if the harships weren't too much to ask of his young bride . . . and Kittie."[5]

At the outset of their western adventure, Bill Sewall had been characteristically blunt with Roosevelt, and when he began to have more serious doubts about the prospects for the cattle industry, he was not hesitant about sharing his thoughts with his friend and boss. "I think the cattle business has seen its best days and I gave my opinion to Mr. R last fall," he told his brother. "I hope he may not lose but think he stands a chance."[6]

Was Roosevelt in too deep? Sewall worried about the possibility: "I am afraid Mr. Roosevelt was led to believe there was more money in it than he will ever see. I can't find any body yet that has made anything out of a small lot of cattle. They are all backed by wealthy men in the east and . . . some of them that have been at it longest are beginning to squirm."[7]

The cause for this was obvious, in his eyes—the environment was too harsh and there were too many cattle in too small a space. "I will venture to say that the longer it runs the worse off they will be," Sewall offered, "for the grass will be growing scarcer and the cattle will not fatten so well and of course they will not be worth so much and will die more."[8]

By the end of the summer of 1886, much of what Sewall had predicted came to pass. The range cattle business was suffering a severe slump as the area was struck by a devastating drought. What little grass there was was becoming overrun by herds pushed north from Texas, Kansas, and Nebraska, where the drought had hit even harder. Ranchers tried to slaughter and sell their cattle before they declined and died, but this only flooded the markets with beef, and prices plummeted.

"Our whole trouble was that cattle had already begun to fall in price before we started, and they continued to fall," Sewall would say in hindsight. "The truth about it all is that in that country, with the long dry summers and the cold winters, no one but a man who was an experienced ranchman and, at the same time, a sharp businessman could ever have expected to come out ahead of the game, and Roosevelt did not pretend to be a businessman. He never cared about making money and he didn't go to Dakota for the money he expected to make there; he came because he liked the country and he liked the people and he liked the wild, adventurous life. The financial side of the ranch was a side issue with him. He cared more about writing books than he did about business, and I guess he cared even more then about doing something in public life than he cared about either [business or writing]."[9]

When Wilmot Dow took the Elkhorn cattle to Chicago for sale in the fall of 1886, he found that the prices were lower than ever, and so was the ranch's financial return. "It turned out we didn't get as much for them as we paid, to say nothing of the trouble of keeping them,"[10] Sewall reported. Elkhorn took a mighty loss. Medora, too, was hurting. The marquis closed his slaughterhouse, finding his suppliers failing and Chicago packing houses offering the same services at cheaper rates.

The downturn made Sewall all the more eager to get out. By now he was counting the days until the terms of their contract with TR were satisfied. "We have now entered the first of our last two years of exile," he wrote back to Island Falls. "The time was three years. The first expired June 1st 1886 so now we are on our last two years. I am having a good time and mean to as long as I stay but it will be a joyful day when I get back and find you all there."[11]

Though they'd seen it coming, Sewall and Dow took the losses hard. They felt a responsibility to Roosevelt and "wondered if experienced cattlemen might not be serving him better."[12] Finally they decided there was not much they could do either way. "[Dow and I] made up our minds that if Roosevelt was willing, the quicker we got out of there the less money he'd lose."

Roosevelt understood full well that the ranch's outlook was bleak, and he didn't want to stand in the way of his friends. "How soon can you go?"[13] he asked.

In October of 1886, the Sewalls and Dows left as quickly as they came, packing up and heading out in a whirlwind ten days. Despite their eagerness to return to Maine, the last days at Elkhorn were ones of sadness. Both Sewalls had mixed feelings. Mary's first reaction was relief and joy, according to her biographer, "and then the thought that they would probably never see this home into which William had built so much of himself made her regretful. . . . their friends . . . the cowboys . . . and the horses that she loved. She was very sorry, too, that Theodore's hopes had not succeeded."[14]

Even though Sewall had privately—and at great length—confided to his brother his less than enthusiastic feelings about the landscape and life in the Badlands, he had very much enjoyed his time with Roosevelt, and he felt a certain accomplishment simply in the construction of the infrastructure at Elkhorn, so he wasn't wholly elated to leave. And when he looked back on the experience later in life he saw only the positives.

Roosevelt actually left the ranch a day ahead of the Sewalls and the Dows. The night before he began his journey back east, he and Bill had a long talk, standing out alone on the prairie. "We were very close in those days and he talked over about everything with me," Sewall remembered. "His ideas and mine always seemed to run about the same."[15]

The young TR again found himself at a juncture, and again he was unsure of the direction he wanted to go. A large part of him wanted to stay and run the ranch. But already there were pressures to return to New York. During his trips back to the city, he had renewed his friendship with his childhood chum Edith Carow, and now it had blossomed into something more than friendship. He also had built a seaside home at Oyster Bay, his famous Sagamore Hill, which would become the site of so many happy Roosevelt summers. He had purchased the 155 acres on Long Island's north shore in 1880, and he and Alice had planned to build there before she died. Shortly after Alice's passing, Bamie had convinced him he needed a place to raise his daughter, and construction was begun. Completed in 1885, his spectacular new home near the city gave him another strong reason to leave the Badlands. He was torn.

His sister Corinne wrote of the moment: "Theodore Roosevelt, however, was not to be allowed by his country to remain too long the rider and dreamer under cottonwood-trees, or even a potent influence for good in Western affairs, as he became. Already rumors were abroad that he would be the choice of the Republican party for the nominee for mayor of New York City. . . ."[16]

If he did return to New York, though, TR wasn't sure politics was what he wanted to pursue. He'd had a job offer to run the New York City Board of Health, but he thought he'd instead like to continue with his study of law, and with the successful publication of his second book, *Hunting Trips of a Ranchman*, in 1885, he thought he could make more money writing than doing anything else.

When asked, Sewall was never without advice: "I told him that he would make a good lawyer, but I should advise him to go into politics because such men as he didn't go into politics, and they were needed in politics." He thought TR would succeed on whatever path he took, and that he could climb as high on the mountain of politics as he wanted: "If you do go into politics and live, your chance to be President is good."

Roosevelt was skeptical. "Bill, you have a lot more faith in me than I have in myself," he replied with a hearty laugh. "That looks a long ways ahead for me."[17]

The pair didn't see each other again for sixteen years.

Daguerreotype portraits of Bill Sewall's parents, Levi and Rebecca, probably made between 1845 and 1855.

Donna Davidge-Bonham / Sewall House

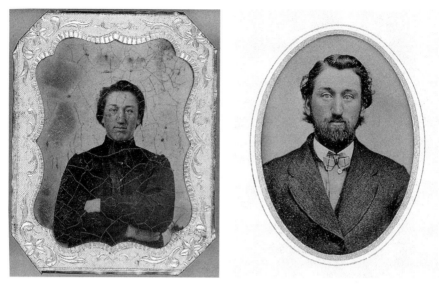

Bill Sewall at sixteen (left) and about age thirty (right)

Sewall kept personal diaries for much of his life.

SATURDAY, JANUARY 7, 1871.

very [illegible] as yet
[illegible] 163 [illegible]
this week

SUNDAY 8

a very pleasant day
and very cold
went to Sherman
broke my sleigh
and raised the
Devil

MONDAY 9

broke our sled
and repaired dam-
ages in the even-
ing a very cold day
and evening

Mary Sewall, Bill's wife, about 1900

Mary and Bill (on right) posed in 1913 with daughter Harriett
(far left), her husband, George Harmon, and their two children.
Standing beside Bill is his eldest daughter, Kittie (in center).

Both photos from Donna Davidge-Bonham / Sewall House

In the 1860s, only a few other buildings stood between the Sewall House (on the left, above) and the Island Falls bridge. For years, it was the only guest house in Island Falls and also served as the post office. After Theodore Roosevelt was elected president, the town landmark became a subject worthy of a picture postcard (below).

Donna Davidge-Bonham / Sewall House

ISLAND FALLS, MAINE. RESIDENCE OF WM. W. SEWELL, EX-PRESIDENT ROOSEVELT'S MAINE GUIDE

Young Theodore Roosevelt in May 1878, a few months before his first trip to Island Falls.

Theodore Roosevelt Collection, Harvard College Library (520.12-005)

Bill Sewall, Wilmot Dow, and Teddy Roosevelt in Maine, March 1879.

Theodore Roosevelt Collection, Harvard College Library (520.12-015)

Wilmot Dow, Bill Sewall's nephew and fellow North Woods guide, accompanied Roosevelt on some of his Maine hunting trips and went to the Dakota Territory with Sewall to run the Elkhorn Ranch.

Donna Davidge-Bonham / Sewall House

Not all of the Maine guide's "sports" wanted a North Woods experience as rugged as Roosevelt chose for himself. Here Sewall (back row, center) and Dow serve up an al fresco lunch to a camping party in 1882.

Donna Davidge-Bonham / Sewall House

My dear Sewall: —

We, the boys, hope you'll receive a small package that we send you, at the same time with this, by express.

In it you'll find a copy of Longfellow for yourself from Mist. A package of tobacco from Mist for Mr. Pingrey. A copy of the Fur Country from myself for you. The rest of the package is the joint contribution—

By the way did the Hogag who took us to Mattawam- keag get home safely? we believed he was going on a grand spree.

An 1879 missive from Arthur Cutler, with a postscript from Emlen Roosevelt, is an example of the steady exchange of letters, gifts, and North Woods mementoes between the Roosevelt and Sewall households.

Donna Davidge-Bonham / Sewall House

very truly yours

Arthur H. Cutler

Dec. 15th 1879
No. 20 W. 43d St.
New York City

P.S. If after supplying Cutler
you could get a couple of
bear skins not costing more
than fifteen dollars apiece
for me I should be much
obliged. With heartiest wishes
for a merry Christmas
and Happy New Year for

all at Island Fall Farm
Very truly yours
T. R. Roosevelt.

P.S. No 2. My fishing rod has
come safely to hand. What
is Captain Sewalls address.
T.R.

SCHOOL FOR BOYS

20 West 43d St.

NEW YORK........ Feb. 16/84

My dear Sewall;—

Theodore's mother died on Thursday morning at 3 A.M. His wife died the same day at 10 A.M. about twenty four hours after the birth of a daughter. Of course the family are utterly demoralized & Theodore is in a dazed, stunned state. He does not know what he does or says.

Arthur Cutler's February 16, 1884, letter informed the Sewalls that Roosevelt's mother and wife had died within hours of each other four days earlier, the event that prompted TR to head to the Badlands.

Donna Davidge-Bonham / Sewall House

I misinformed you.
Nat was not married
last month but is to
be the 26th of February.
This matter of course
makes his wedding very
simple quiet.

The funeral for both the
Mrs. Roosevelt took place
this morning, a very sad
sight.   The Legislature
has adjourned for three
days out of respect for
Theodore's loss.

The box of skins has arrived, I'll
attend to the matter next week.

yours truly

Arthur H. Cutter

123

Souvenir postcard showing the cabin at Chimney Butte Ranch in present-day North Dakota where Roosevelt stayed while Bill Sewall and Wilmot Dow were building the house at Elkhorn Ranch.

Donna Davidge-Bonham / Sewall House

Roosevelt reenacted one of his most famous Badlands escapades for the camera. Above: TR guards the captive thieves, played by Sewall (standing), Dow, and an unidentified ranch hand. Right: Dow and Sewall in the boat Sewall built to pursue the miscreants downriver.

Donna Davidge-Bonham / Sewall House

Right to left: Mary Sewall holding Kittie, Lizzie Dow, and two other women (identified as a Mrs. Tisdale and a Miss Wadsworth) enjoy an outing at Elkhorn Ranch. Horseback riding was one of the few diversions that brightened Mary's lonely days in the Dakota Territory.

Donna Davidge-Bonham / Sewall House

A promotional photo made in 1885, when Roosevelt's *Hunting Trips of a Ranchman* was published. TR was proud of his buckskins.

Theodore Roosevelt Collection, Harvard College Library (520.14-002)

A studio portrait of Bill Sewall, during his cowboy days

Donna Davidge-Bonham / Sewall House

Dec 28th '93

Friend William,

Here is no one from whom I am more glad to hear than from you; and there is no one who rejoices more sincerely over your good fortune than I do. It may be some time yet, but surely, sooner or later, I am going to bring my family up to ___ a few weeks on the lake.

In a December 1893 letter to Sewall, Roosevelt mentions his desire to return to Island Falls, a common theme in his correspondence.

Donna Davidge-Bonham / Sewall House

Yes, I *did* have a savage first time of it here with that unreconstructed rebel, old Johnston. He, was a real type of the fire-eater; he always went armed with a revolver, and was always bullying and threatening and talking about his deeds as a General in the War, and "his people" the Southerners, and "his party" the Democrats. He was a big fellow, and once or twice I wished I had your thews; but as I hadn't, I resolved to what I could with my own, if it came to a rough and tumble. However, he was like the Marquis, that time he wrote me the note when we were all at the ranch. After he had carried his bullying to a certain point I brought him up with a round turn, and when he threatened I told him to go right ahead, that I was no brawler, but that I was always ready to defend myself in any way, and that moreover I would guarantee to do it, too. Then he backed off. I was always having difficulties with him as he was an inveterate hater of Republicans in general, of Northerners, and especially of negroes. However, I finally drove him off the Commission; and before this happened I had reduced him to absolute impotence on the Commission, save that he could still be a temporary obstructionist.

I am glad your people and the Dows are in good health and doing well; all my own family are well also. I am well too, though I don't get any exercise now; and this has been a very hard business year. Your friend
Theodore Roosevelt

Cover and interior page from a promotional brochure
for Bill Sewall's sporting camps
Donna Davidge-Bonham / Sewall House

"Stairway of Anticipation" Hook Point Camps

Sewall began operating Hook Point Camps on Mattawamkeag
Lake in 1903. These photos probably date from the 1920s.

HELPED PRESIDENT BACK TO HEALTH, SO HE'LL GET A FAT JOB

WILLIAM W. SEWELL.

"Bill" Sewell Has Grown Village
Weary of Sorting
Mail Wherefore His Friend,
Theodore Roosevelt, Will
Call Him Higher.

do. Sorting the mail of his neighbors is not to his liking, so last March
he took a trip to Washington to see
the President. He came away assured
that his wishes would be granted.

Sewell is a typical Maine woodsman
and is the first white person born in
this town. In 1880, when Roosevelt was
a student at Harvard College and became so ill that his physicians said he
could not recover, Sewell invited the

Special to the Post-Dispatch.

Some newspaper editors tried to cast Sewall's 1905 federal appointment as collector of customs in a nepotistic light.

Donna Davidge-Bonham / Sewall House

This photo probably dates from Bill Sewall's fourth and last trip to Washington, in March 1909, when friends and dignitaries—the president's "Tennis Cabinet"—gathered to honor Theodore Roosevelt during his last days in the White House. Sewall is sixth from right.

Donna Davidge-Bonham / Sewall House

On the front porch of the Sewall House, 1920s

Donna Davidge-Bonham / Sewall House

Futures and Fame

When Bill Sewall arrived back in Maine, he would get his first taste of what his life would be like into the future. People at the train station in Portland had heard that William Sewall and his family were returning from their cowboy adventure in the Wild West, and when the train pulled in, crowds gathered to hear their stories. The scene was repeated at every stop in Maine. Mary remembered Bill talking to anyone and everyone, charming them with tales of their adventures and escapades on the frontier. He already seemed to be ignoring the difficulties they had faced on the ranch, recalling only the good times. He would introduce the children riding on his and Wilmot's shoulders as the "Badlands babies."[1]

Between stations, the Sewalls looked longingly out the window as they chugged their way north, drinking in the "green grass, rivers and lakes of sweet water, white birches and pointed evergreens as a wanderer on the desert greets an oasis," as Mary's biographer would put it.[2] When they finally reached Island Falls they were met with more excitement—all their friends and family eager to see them once again and to hear the stories of cowboy life.

Bill and Mary Sewall moved back into the Sewall House and resumed life largely as they left it. Bill was up at dawn the day after they returned to check on the status of the house, his barn and buildings, and his woodlot. His brothers Dave and Sam had looked after the property well, even finishing a shed that Bill had started before he was called to meet Roosevelt in New York. The brothers conferred on what had been accomplished, and Dave peppered Bill with questions about life on the ranch.

There was much catching up to do with the day-to-day goings-on in Island Falls, too. The town now had more than two hundred residents, and continued to grow, with the new Emerson General Store opening in 1887. But learning everything that had been happening didn't take long when the local post office was in your front room. And everyone was eager to meet Fred, the Badlands baby.

Bill and Sam started up again in the woods that winter, hauling logs and cutting railroad ties. Wilmot reopened his blacksmith shop just south of the bridge at the center of town. Over the next few years he had two more sons, George and

Levi.[3] Summer found Sewall at work on the farm, and when he and Dow could make the time, the pair tramped off into the woods, hunting and fishing. Bill stole moments with his kids whenever he could. As Mary's biographer described it, "he cherished his time with them and often kept them by his side even when it slowed what he was doing."[4]

As the months went on, Bill and Mary would get frequent letters from Roosevelt. He was having a more difficult time extricating himself from the West. TR may have left on an earlier train than the Sewalls, but he was still deeply vested in the Dakota Territory, and he seemed much more reluctant to put away his buckskins for good. He kept making trips back out West, but didn't pour any more significant sums into his old dream, especially after he had remarried and started a new family. He loaned the remainder of the Elkhorn herd to his neighbors Ferris and Merrifield in a fifty-fifty arrangement, and he would continue to have money invested in ranching—paying taxes on a herd of cattle—until 1898.

Like the Sewalls in Maine, Roosevelt had settled back into life in the East. He had changed markedly during his time at Elkhorn with the Sewalls. "He went to Dakota a frail young man, suffering from asthma and stomach trouble," Sewall would remember. "When he got back into the world again, he was as husky as almost any man I have ever seen who wasn't dependent on his arms for his livelihood. He weighed one hundred and fifty pounds, and was clear bone, muscle, and grit. . . . physically strong enough to be anything he wanted from President of the United States on down."[5]

Sewall wasn't the only one to notice. A friend of Roosevelt's from Harvard was surprised to bump into TR on the street in New York: "I recall my astonishment the first time I saw him, after the lapse of several years, to find him with the neck of a Titan and with broad shoulders and stalwart chest, instead of the city-bred, slight young friend I had known earlier."[6]

One of the reasons Roosevelt had elected to return to New York was to run for mayor of the city. He did so in 1886 and lost, but, as he said to Bill Sewall, it wasn't a job he wanted anyway. Several months later, in 1887, he published the book he'd been working on so diligently at Elkhorn—*The Life of Thomas Hart Benton*, which would be his third title. Benton, a senator from Missouri, had spent much of his career arguing the merits of westward expansion—the Manifest Destiny of the day—a subject also dear to his biographer. While a lieutenant colonel in the army, Benton had gained notoriety for getting in a brawl with Andrew Jackson. Though well educated, he had a populist streak and, like Roosevelt, felt an affinity for the rugged frontiersman. And Roosevelt would continue to work on writing projects, when he wasn't running off to board meetings or charitable functions.

But his chief interest when he again took up residence in New York in the autumn of 1886 was Edith Kermit Carow. The pair had known each other since they were in knickers, playing house together as young as five, and Carow was a close friend of his sisters. When he was traveling through Europe on his family's grand tour at eight, he'd write home to Edith, calling her his "most faithful correspondent."[7] Years later at Harvard, almost as if to hedge his bets when he was courting Alice, he'd ask in his letters to Bamie and Corinne to be remembered to her. These missives were often laced with innuendo. "When you write to Edith," he asked Conie, "tell her I enjoyed *her* visit *very* much indeed."[8]

Edith subscribed to the convention of the time that "A woman's name should appear in print but twice—when she's married and when she's buried,"[9] and hers made the news on December 2, 1886, when she was wedded to her childhood friend at St. George's Church, Hanover Square, London.

Roosevelt had barreled into his second courtship the same way he'd started his ranch, wasting little time on tedious formalities. Back in New York, the society columnists took notice, sniffing in the *New York Times's* "Society Topics of the Week" column that the engagement was only two months long and that the marriage might strike some to have come "somewhat prematurely."[10]

Though the Sewalls and Dows had left Elkhorn that fall and the outlook for his cattle venture seemed bleak, Roosevelt identified himself in the wedding register as "twenty-eight, widower, ranchman."[11] And the goings-on along the Little Missouri were still in the back of his mind as he and his new bride embarked on their honeymoon, traveling across Europe. When he later heard about a disastrous winter in the American West, he hurried home to go check on the state of the ranch.

In Island Falls, Sewall waited for word himself. News from Elkhorn was rarely good, and the situation that winter could rightly be called a disaster. The guide's first observation in the Badlands must have been ringing in Roosevelt's ears. On April 7, 1887, Sewall got a letter from TR apprising him of the situation.

"You were mighty lucky to leave when you did," Roosevelt wrote. "This spring I should have had to rustle pretty hard to pay your fare back. By all accounts the loss among the cattle has been terrible. About the only comfort that I have out of it is that at any rate you and Wilmot are all right; I would not mind the loss of a few thousands, if it was the only way to benefit you and Will—but it will be much more than that. I am going out west in a few days to look at things for myself."[12]

The cold was severe and the snow was deep, and thousands upon thousands of animals were lost, many of them freezing where they stood. Blizzards began at the end of November, when twenty inches fell, and the harsh weather continued all winter. In December there were twenty-one days when the low temperature stayed below zero, and for more than half of the month the mercury fell to minus twenty or worse. It never relented.[13] By spring the Dakota herd was decimated—75 percent of the region's cattle dropped in barns and pastures.[14]

That April, Roosevelt and his business partner at Chimney Butte, William Merrifield, went for a scouting trip to see how their brand fared. It was bad. "Well, you can not imagine anything more dreary than the look of the Badlands when I went out there," TR wrote Sewall. "Everything was cropped as bare as a bone, the sagebrush had been eaten down until the stems were as thick as my two fingers; the bush was just fed out by the starving cattle. . . . In almost every coulee there was dead cattle. There were nearly three hundred on Wadsworth bottom."[15]

Roosevelt felt the losses deeply. He told his friend Henry Cabot Lodge that he was "for the first time utterly unable to enjoy a visit to my ranch."[16] And to Bamie he wrote, "I am bluer than indigo about the cattle." He might not have gotten into ranching to make a fortune, but he was certainly feeling the financial losses. "I wish I was sure I'd lose no more than half the money ($80,000) I invested out here. I am planning how to get out of it."[17]

In the fall of 1889 he sent another note to Sewall. "I am picking up a little in the cattle business," he said, "branding a slightly larger number of calves each year, and putting back a few thousand dollars into my capital; but I shall never make good my losses."[18]

Sewall and Dow occasionally heard from other friends on the Little Missouri as well. In a letter written at the end of March in 1888, Howard Eaton, another transplanted Easterner who fell in love with the West, told Sewall that many of the men on neighboring ranches—including Joe Ferris—were looking to get out of the cattle business or relocate their operations to greener pastures. Literally. It was an extensive list; "Martin has gone to Helena. Tom McGregor, Tom Martin, Fred Herring, Billy Smith, Jack Sawyer, Walter Watterson, and I believe Bill Rowe are in or near Helena. The Thompkins family have quite vanished from public gaze—at least around Medora. Lew Hunt closed out last fall and is in Duluth, in the real estate business. Harry Bennet killed a man in some row in Illinois or Indiana."[19]

Indeed, the Sewalls received plenty of correspondence from old friends in New York and later Washington, sometimes from Arthur Cutler, sometimes from Emlen or West Roosevelt. (The letters Sewall received from Emlen Roosevelt often expressed a single desire: "I have still hopes that some day I may get a chance to run up and see you," he wrote in February of 1904, "but I have been disappointed so often that I do not feel as sure as I did at first.")

But most of the letters came from Roosevelt himself. Their friendship, once built on physical pursuits, became an epistolary one—letters to "Friend William" made a steady march north over the decades. At first they were filled with talk of the ranch, but they also included everything from hunting tales to political talk. In one missive there is an intriguing hint that Sewall had requested a loan, which Roosevelt declined.[20] (The letter, unfortunately, includes no details about why Sewall wanted the loan or why Roosevelt decided against it.)

In all this correspondence, TR covered a wide territory. In one letter he wondered about an apocryphal tale about a Sewall who killed a moose with an ax (he had read an account of such a thing and thought it was probably impossible, but had this idea he'd heard that one of Bill's brothers claimed this feat on his résumé). He frequently asked after Sewall's mother and sister and asked to be remembered to Mary and Lizzie ("Do Mrs. Sewall and Mrs. Dow ever think of the old ranch house?") and "all of my friends" in Island Falls.[21]

Sometimes the letters would come addressed jointly to Bill and Wilmot, like the note Roosevelt mailed on the day after Christmas in 1887, thanking his guides for the gift basket and toy canoe they sent.[22] The Sewalls sent presents on an annual basis, everything from socks to pants to the Roosevelts' favorite—maple sugar candy—and many letters from TR mention his appreciation. Mary and Lizzie and Bill's mother had started a tradition of knitting socks for Roosevelt— he had been impressed with Mary's "speed and accuracy"[23] at Elkhorn— and he continued to request them, even sending samples to show what he'd like, while he was in the White House.

Once Roosevelt described how he was having a difficult time with a particular individual during his Civil Service days: "He was a big fellow, and once or twice I wished I had your thews; but, as I had not, I resolved to [do] what I could with my own if it came to rough and tumble."[24]

Another theme that recurred endlessly in their correspondence was the New Yorker's yearning to return to the woods and waters of Mattawamkeag. "How I wish you and I and Will were going on a hunt together now!"[25] Roosevelt thought that closing the ranch would help things along—"and then if I get any hunting it will have to be in Maine."[26]

He not only hoped to return to Maine himself, but as his family expanded he very much hoped his children would have the opportunity to travel and learn with Sewall guidance. In a letter sent in May of 1888 he said he thought his infant son Theodore, Jr., "ought to take to the woods kindly, for the little canoe you sent him is one of his favorite toys; I'll guess in the future I will have to turn him loose in Aroostook County now and then, under the tuition of yours and Wilmot's sons."[27] After Kermit was born a year later, it was much the same: "[B]oth of my boys will in the future make the acquaintance of Island Falls and I hope will learn to trap muskrats and shoot ducks and partridges. . . ."[28]

The postman carried letters south as well, and Roosevelt was always eager to receive word from Island Falls. In the "Congressional Gossip" column of the *Bryan Times*, on March 19, 1903, TR says as much. This was after he became President and a dozen or so senators had called on him to discuss a post that was about to be filled. Instead they found "Mr. Roosevelt more inclined to discuss 'Bill' Sewall, the celebrated Maine guide, from whom he had just received a letter." The Congressmen attempted to capture the President's attention, but were unable to do so. Finally someone said, "Mr. President, you seem very much interested in this guide." Roosevelt responded, "Yes, Senator, I am. 'Bill' is an interesting man and a real friend. He is the only man in the United States, who on writing the President about an office, or anything else, addresses him as 'Friend, Theodore.'"[29]

But that particular incident was years down the road. Roosevelt still had to make his entrance onto the world stage, and that occurred in 1898, the year after he was appointed assistant secretary of the navy by President McKinley. The Spanish were asserting themselves in territory Roosevelt considered vital to American interests—the Caribbean. Simply put—and TR did tend to see things in stark contrasts— Roosevelt believed they should stop. But if they wanted a fight, he would be glad to give them one.

Whenever Theodore Roosevelt was looking at a serious bit of rough and tumble, his thoughts invariably returned to Bill Sewall. In this instance, his friend didn't disagree with the politics involved in going to war with Spain, nor did he have a problem with fighting per se, but he opposed TR's personal involvement. "I was one of those who thought he had no business himself to go to war," he later explained. "I never was a pacifist in my life anymore than he was. Neither of us wanted to pick a quarrel, but when a quarrel came, we weren't the men to dodge it." Sewall just didn't think Roosevelt's best service to the nation would be as a soldier. "It seemed to me, however, that it wasn't his place to go to Cuba. I thought he had more important work to do in the Navy Department and I wrote him so."[30]

Roosevelt sent a reply "as quick as the mails could carry it,"[31] and asked Sewall to saddle up. Amused, Sewall responded that he was a graying fifty-three by this point, not quite as tall or strong as he had been when they first met. TR wrote him again, saying, "Come on, anyway. You are worth half a regiment with your knowledge of woodcraft."[32]

When Sewall declined, Roosevelt sent him yet another note. "There is no man whose good wishes I value more than yours," he asserted. "I just couldn't keep out of this fight." And he teased Sewall that he didn't really expect him to come. "No, there will be no need for you, and you would have no business to leave your home; but I am willing to bet half I'm worth that there won't be in all my regiment, young men though they will be, a single man as tough and hardy and able to give a good account of himself, as you."[33]

Once war was declared, Sewall eagerly followed the news and was immensely proud when he learned of the heroics of Colonel Roosevelt and his Rough Riders, and he "told of Theodore's exploits as long as he lived."[34] He wasn't the only one in town. Many in the community had met Theodore Roosevelt and were keenly following the dispatches from Cuba. It might have been a short war, but in Island Falls every development was watched closely.

Whoever was at the pen—be it Sewall or Roosevelt—was never at a shortage for news. And, of course, it wasn't always as triumphant as the bulletins about the exploits of the Rough Riders at San Juan Hill. As the Sewall family grew with the births of his children Harriet in 1888 and Merrill in 1891, the proud father wrote to his friend. When it contracted, with the death of Bill's mother in October of 1891, two months after Merrill's birth, he wrote again. At the age of ninety, Rebecca Sewall had succumbed to dysentery caused by cholera.

Earlier that year, the Sewalls had suffered another loss, one that hit everyone, including Roosevelt, particularly hard.

That spring, Bill and Wilmot were working on a river drive in the employ of Wilbur Grant. Grant was a businessman from Kingman, a small community thirty-five miles south of Island Falls, and he had contracted with Sewall to buy railroad ties. Pleased with how things had turned out, Grant then hired the guide to oversee his crew, and Sewall, in turn, brought his nephew along. Dow had spent the winter looking forward to it. Once they were on site, though, deep in the woodlands, he began to feel ill. The sickness stayed with him for days, and finally he left to see a doctor. He began to lose weight rapidly, and none of the area's physicians could determine what the cause was. Then suddenly he was gone, at age thirty-six, widowing his wife and leaving behind three sons. Sewall would later come to the conclusion that he died of acute Bright's disease—the same kidney ailment that took Alice Roosevelt—and that he had begun to suffer from it back in the Dakotas.

Bill Sewall was devastated. "His death was such a blow to us as I cannot describe," he'd later write. Everywhere he went in Island Falls the memories of Will were triggered; Sewall couldn't escape them even in his favorite sanctuary. "The woods and waters and all nature was constant reminder of him." The pain was so much that Sewall put down his rod and reel for years. He wouldn't pick them up again for pleasure "until my own sons were old enough to be taught to fish and hunt."[35]

Roosevelt, too, was deeply saddened. He wrote Sewall in May, "I cannot realize that he, so lusty and powerful and healthy, can have gone. You know how highly I esteemed Wilmot. He was one of the men whom I felt proud to have as a friend and he has left his children the name of an upright and honorable man who played his part manfully in the world. His sincerity and strength of character, his courage, his gentleness to his wife, his loyalty to his friends, all made him one whose loss must be greatly mourned. . . . May we all do our duty as straightforwardly and well as he did his."[36]

Four months later, in August, when he sent Sewall a note about the birth of his daughter Ethel, TR was still mourning Dow: "I think of Wilmot all the time. I can see him riding a bucker or paddling a canoe, or shooting an antelope; or doing the washing for his wife, or playing with the children. If ever there was a fine, noble fellow, he was one."[37] (Roosevelt also asked Sewall to see if Mrs. Dow would sell him Wilmot's Sharps 40-90 rifle.[38])

Upon his return from a hunting trip in Africa in 1892, Roosevelt remarked to Sewall that Dow was the surest shot he'd ever seen. When he arranged to buy Wilmot's gun from Lizzie, his intention was to make an heirloom of it—he wanted his boys to know from whom it came, to know, as he told Sewall, "all about Wilmot and you."[39]

Much as his friend Theodore Roosevelt had done before him, Bill Sewall tried to quell his grief by diving into strenuous activity, and he had plenty to keep him busy. In her biography of Mary Sewall, Harriet Miller described how Bill drew his family into yet another new venture. At the breakfast table one morning in 1892, his eyes gleaming, he told his wife about a development that would again change their lives: that afternoon he would be conferring with a railroad engineer he'd met in Lincoln the previous week.

That teams of laborers were pushing the railroad through the wilderness north of Mattawamkeag was hardly news to Mary. Ever since the train had come to Mattawamkeag, Sewall had been working toward the goal of extending the line through the woodlands to Island Falls, and finally, not long after Wilmot died, crews had begun laying tracks. They wanted to base a construction crew in Island Falls, and Bill had told the railroad man he thought the Sewalls could provide room and board for forty of the workers.

Mary did not share his excitement and demanded to know who was going to do all the cooking. Bill was shocked that she was less than enthusiastic. He explained that boarding the work crew would bring in more money than logging and promised to hire a cookee to help her feed all those hungry men.

This notion didn't ease Mary's mind any either. To appease her, Sewall considered putting up just five or six men, but in the end he decided that taking more would be just too profitable to pass up. Also, it was a point of pride with him that Sewalls didn't turn away people looking for a place to stay. In the words of their granddaughter, Harriet Miller, Bill and Mary were known for "the warmth of their hospitality and the quality of their generous meals."[40]

The episode was disturbing to Mary not only because it represented a lot of work—and infinite patience—but because for the first time it made her question the family finances. She'd always thought of the Sewall enterprise as fairly self-sufficient. They grew or hunted most of the food they ate. Their house was warmed by wood Bill cut. She made much of their clothing. But as the ways of Island Falls life slowly became more sophisticated, certain necessities—such as train travel—required actual money. Mary had no idea how much they had. Bill carried some bills around in a roll and kept some cash in a safe at home, but how much? He was always very generous in helping out those he could—if someone needed a down payment for a mortgage, for example—and he gave whenever a community enterprise was seeking support. They even had a hired girl who helped her with cooking, cleaning, and the children. But did they have enough to stay solvent in the changing world?

As it turned out, Bill wasn't able to locate the cook he promised—they were all hired out already "in the boom town Island Falls had become"—and soon the Sewall House was overflowing with hearty appetites. The stately home Sewall had constructed for his father was big—a dozen rooms and two attached barns—but it was nowhere near big enough when the railroad regiment arrived.

When the breakfast bell rang, as Sewall remembered later, "you could see men coming from every conceivable place where there was room enough for a bed or even to place a mattress: from all the chambers, the stable, hayloft, and wagon shed." The task of feeding such a crew—there were actually forty-five men—was monumental, as Mary had anticipated, and she couldn't do it with only the help of one hired girl. So Sewall turned to and did much of the cooking himself. Little Fred would later recall that his parents used a barrel of flour a day for all the baking.[41]

In addition to working in the kitchen, Sewall contracted with the railroad company to drive the twenty-five miles to Houlton three times a week for supplies, and also to transport the weekly payroll cash, not the safest of occupations. He'd already been serving as a deputy county sheriff for about a year, so adding a payroll run to his responsibilities was nothing out of the ordinary for him. He spent so much time on the road that he had to buy an extra pair of horses.

Sewall would spend fifteen years in law enforcement, making many arrests over the years, much as he had in the Finnegan adventure out West. In Maine, however, he never carried a firearm. Most of the time he avoided trouble by sheer dint of his

143

size—nobody wanted to mess with him. "He was surprisingly quick and able at self defense," according to Mary. Still, both she and especially their youngest daughter, Nancy (born in 1894), worried when Bill was on a call. According to granddaughter Harriet, Sewall downplayed dangers, only once telling Mary, "Maybe I had some narrow escapes; but they didn't harm me, only bruised my knuckles."[42]

There were a few memorable scraps. One miscreant named John Donovan supposedly came to Island Falls expressly "to pick a row," setting up at the Exchange Hotel (the town's first formal hostelry, built in 1893) and making a nuisance of himself. The proprietor sent for Sewall. When the big deputy arrived, Donovan was abusive and resisted arrest, much to the excitement of the many onlookers. Sewall wrapped his huge hands around the man's throat and "choked him into submission." Donovan was thrown in the local jail, was tried the next day, and fined sixteen dollars—which Sewall paid for him.

The deputy attempted to befriend another menace, Pat Morin, who had a reputation in Houlton for kicking and trampling men with his spiked logging boots. Supposedly, eight men had once tried to restrain him and failed. When Morin showed up in Island Falls, Sewall thought it best that the famed brawler stay at the Sewall House, where he could be watched. Morin had been a guest for several days when word came down that he was again wanted by the law for something he had done in Houlton. Before Sewall could turn him in, he slipped out of town, but as he did he was reported to have claimed, "You couldn't get away from Bill Sewall, with fingers like iron. . . I didn't want them around my neck."[43]

It was a historic day when the first Bangor and Aroostook train at last tooted its way into the new depot at Island Falls on November 23, 1893. The whole town turned out to celebrate, except Mary Sewall, who was too busy. Bill couldn't have been any more excited,[44] but he would later laugh and remark, "My wife has ever since said that to think of that time is a nightmare."[45] The Island Falls train station was finished in February 1894, and "its metallic ceiling, walls finished in natural wood, and neatly and tastily fitted office" gave it the reputation of being the finest facility on the line from Brownville to Houlton.[46]

The coming of rail led to an era of massive change in the Falls, just as Sewall had envisioned. Between 1893 and 1900 the population grew more than fourfold, from 223 souls to more than a thousand.[47] Bill counted twenty new homes, six stores, eight new industries, including a sawmill and the town's largest employer, Proctor, Hunt, & Co., based in Boston. The company opened a tannery on the Mattawamkeag in 1893, and it would become the largest in New England. This in addition to three new social halls, a pharmacy, a lawyer, a doctor, and a new Congregational Church, which particularly excited Mary Sewall.[48]

Within the next decade the town would see the arrival of electricity and telephones, a dozen more businesses, and a handful of new churches. Sewall was a staunch advocate of progress and worked his entire life to develop the town, but later in life when he reflected on what development brought to Island Falls, he had contradictory thoughts: "Many changes I have seen during my eighty odd years of life, but I do not believe people are any happier now, for all the improvements and new ways, than we were back in the old days."[49]

Much was changing in the life of his friend from New York, too. Bill Sewall was keenly interested in Roosevelt's rise through the ranks of politics. "The first thing I knew," he remarked, "I was writing to a man who was Governor of New York. [TR was elected in 1898, shortly after his well-publicized derring-do with the Rough Riders in Cuba.] We corresponded quite a good deal during those years. He seemed to be interested in getting my point of view on things, and it happened that we always agreed on the fundamental things; just as we had agreed when we were in Maine and Dakota together. I hadn't seen Theodore for twelve years, but our minds seemed to run like a team."[50]

The duties of the office didn't stop the new governor from taking time to dash off notes to his mentor in northern Maine. Two weeks after TR's inauguration as governor, Sewall was pleased to receive a letter confirming that their opinions still ran square with one another. "What you say about the reforms is exactly true," Roosevelt wrote in that 1899 missive. "People like to talk about reform, but they don't want to give one hour's work or five cents worth of time. They would much rather sit at home and grumble at the men who really do the work, because these men, like all others, are sure to make mistakes sometimes."[51]

Roosevelt also laid out his intentions, and to a twenty-first-century reader, his stated plan comes as a surprise. "I've had a pretty busy year," he wrote, "but I have enjoyed it all and I am proud of being Governor and am going to try and make a square and decent one. I do not expect, however, to hold this type of political office again and in one way that is a help, because the politicians cannot threaten me with what they will do in the future."[52]

In his gut Sewall knew the idea of TR withdrawing from public life was unlikely. When a reporter from the *Los Angeles Times* came to Island Falls to pry some colorful stories about New York's new governor out of the former guide, Sewall obliged with a few tales about the Red Finnegan episode and others, then offered this prescient observation: "Well, I suppose he'll have his hands full looking after political pirates from now on. But I know when I go up to Albany to see him seated in the Governor's chair next month, there'll be the same old grasp of the hand, the same hearty welcome for Bill Sewall, and I expect to see the day when Theodore Roosevelt will reign at the White House."[53]

I Want to See Roosevelt

One August day in 1902, Mary looked out the window of the Sewall House to see her husband hurrying home. As her biographer noted, Mary could tell from his face that something was up. As soon as he saw her, Bill exclaimed, "Theodore is coming to Bangor. He'd like to see us there!"[1] Now a gray fifty-seven, the guide who had proven himself able to keep his cool under the most difficult of circumstances was ebullient.

It shouldn't have been any surprise that Theodore Roosevelt wanted to see his old friend. He said so in just about every letter he wrote. But now he was actually coming—he'd said so himself. And he wasn't just "Theodore" or "Mr. Roosevelt" any more. He wasn't the governor or even the vice president. He was the president of the United States, having taken office the previous autumn when William McKinley was assassinated by an anarchist in Buffalo. (Typical of TR, he received the news of McKinley's death when he was finishing a climb of Mount Marcy, the highest peak in the Adirondacks.[2])

"Goodness, William," Mary exclaimed, "I thought somebody died."

"It's just as important as somebody dying," he replied. "The President of the United States is coming to Bangor! And it's Theodore! Sixteen years since we said goodbye to him in Medora. . . . Now he is doing things that he had talked about during those long Dakota evenings."[3]

Sewall was excited, but he wasn't really caught unawares. The *New York Times* had published a piece at the end of June that mentioned an impending visit Roosevelt would pay to Bangor, and Sewall surely knew about it, because he'd been interviewed for the story. Titled "Roosevelt's Old Guide," it contained a long conversation with "Bill" and credited him with making a man out of the young Harvard student. And it had declared that the Aroostook man would be "among the thousands who will welcome President Roosevelt when he comes to Bangor in August."[4]

Perhaps he had been a tad skeptical, though, because word that Roosevelt would visit the Pine Tree State had circulated back when he was vice president, and it had proved untrue. At the time, Sewall inquired about the trip in one of his letters, and Roosevelt dashed his hopes: "There is not any truth in the rumor that I am going up to Maine this year. If I ever do, you may be certain that I shall come straight to your house."[5]

Sewall didn't tell the president, but he was certainly planning to be there for the event. "I suppose he knew that I would be there, just the same as I knew he would be looking for me," Sewall would say later. Dressed in a jacket and uncomfortable white collar, he took the morning train to the Queen City and set up at the Bangor House, the city's most famous hostelry and one of the last great palace hotels in the East. His family would join him later, if Mary could finish the chores in time.

While the old guide was waiting in Bangor, he was spotted by Llewellyn Powers, of Houlton, the congressman from Maine's second district, who asked if he was going to go see the president speak at the fairgrounds. The Island Falls man told him there was no use in going. "I want to see Roosevelt," he allowed. "If I go down there, I shall not be able to because there will be so many of you fellows around him." Instead, Sewall asked his congressman to tell TR where he was. "I'll be sitting right here."[6] And sit there he did.

A huge crowd gathered to see the young president and hear him speak. It had been the same in Augusta and Waterville. Roosevelt's visit to Maine was the first by any president in years, and area employers gave workers the day off to mark the occasion. They arrived in the thousands and roared when the new president appeared.

"Teddy" held up his hand for silence. "You want me to speak," he said, "but I've come out here simply to act as my own town crier. There is a man in Maine who I haven't seen in years, but whom I particularly want to see now.

"Is Bill Sewall in town? Has anyone seen him? Does anyone know where he is? I would you would tell him, if you do, that I would like to renew old times with him. Tell him I'll be disappointed if he doesn't come."

Congressman Powers went and fetched the guide. "The president wants to see you," he told Sewall. "He has asked for you in every town in which he has stopped in Maine."

By this time, Mary and the children had arrived, accompanied by Wilmot Dow's widow, Lizzie, and her new husband, Fleetwood Pride. When they finally met, President Roosevelt went right down the line, greeting each one in turn. As the *New York Times* reported it, Roosevelt said, "I am glad to see you, Bill," and Sewall replied, with tears in his eyes, "You ain't no gladder than I be."[7] Then, "while others waited," it was hello to Mary, Lizzie and Pride, and Bill's daughter Harriet. Roosevelt asked after Bill's brothers Sam and Dave, and gave a special nod to the youngest member of the party: "Little Harriet, I'm glad to see you!"[8] And he launched into one of his favorite stories about Fred and Wilmot on the ranch, before the Secret Service men escorted him away.

Bill later sat near the presidential party at another speech at the Bangor Fair Grounds, and that was the last his wife saw of him that day—he disappeared. Mary assumed he had tagged along with the thousands of others to see the President off to his train, and that night she and Harriet stayed at the hotel and waited for Bill's return, but he never showed. After waiting and worrying all the next day, she decided to take the train home to Island Falls, where she continued to fret.

Two days later Bill came home with an explanation for his vanishing act. He'd been invited to ride on the president's train for the remainder of the tour through Maine and New Hampshire. The pair fell in so naturally it was as if the sixteen summers that had passed were days rather than years. During their first dinner together since Elkhorn, President Roosevelt proceeded to recount many of the pair's adventures to the assembled gathering, including the time, on his third trip into the woods with Sewall, when they had to eat muskrat because they'd run out of food and the rodent was all the game they could bag. It was the last meat he'd eaten in Maine.

The *New York Tribune* published a lengthy report of the reunion, titled "Old 'Bill' Sewall the Most Enthusiastic Roosevelt Man in Maine." As the article described it, "When the celebration at Bangor, Me., in honor of President Roosevelt's visit, was over, many of the people of that town wondered who was the greater lion, the President or 'Old Bill' Sewall. The latter was the most conspicuous figure in the day's proceedings, not because he obtruded himself on the public, but because the President asked to have him near him."

"If 'Old Bill' Sewall is in town," said Mr. Roosevelt, "I want him to join me at luncheon, for I feel like a man who has lost his partner in a crowd."

"Twas all we could do to help having a holding match," Sewall is quoted as saying. The reporter continued: "No meeting of two brothers long separated could have been more pathetic than the meeting of the President and the rough woodsman. The old man had the day of his life."[9]

After his speech at the Bangor Fair Grounds, during which he preached morality to a nation he thought needed it, Roosevelt had asked Sewall to dinner and invited the guide to ride with him on the remainder of his trip.

According to the newspaper account, at one point, Sewall looked at Roosevelt and asked him if he recalled their last evening on the prairie. "Do you remember what I told you," he asked, "here in Maine and in Dakota?"

"Yes. How strange you knew," replied TR.

"It was not strange to me," Bill said. "I did not expect to see you made President this way. That is, I didn't suppose you would be shot into the Presidency, but I expected to see you become President in a different manner and I expect you to, yet. We will do that, next time."[10]

The pair spent hours catching up, and during the course of their conversation, Roosevelt told Sewall that the endless tramps they'd taken through the woods together—tests of endurance and stamina—had been just what he needed. Sewall mentioned this to a reporter: "When the President used to come up here he'd be the best fellow always. He could put up with anything, and he told me to-day that it has done him a lot of good, though he hain't as healthy now as he was then."[11]

The long-lost soulmates were hard to separate, but when they at last parted ways, Roosevelt promised, "We'll break bread in the White House."[12]

Just days later, a letter from 1600 Pennsylvania Avenue arrived in Island Falls. In it Roosevelt thanked Mrs. Sewall and Mrs. Pride for the socks they'd knitted him, and he made good on his word, extending a formal invitation for the Sewalls to visit the White House. Roosevelt wanted to see everyone; Sewall later recalled that TR told him to bring "my family and my two brothers and their families and Mrs. Pride and her husband . . . . I think he asked twenty-five of us in all."[13]

The president was hosting a judicial reception at the end of January and a congressional reception in February, and he thought his guide would find both events interesting, adding, "I think the Congressional Reception you would probably enjoy most." Roosevelt then explained that he'd have his personal assistant meet them at their train, make arrangements for their hotel, escort them to the White House, and "show them all the sights." At the bottom of the typed letter Roosevelt scrawled in his own handwriting, "Come sure, we'll have a celebration."[14]

Another letter followed in September, prodding the guide again: "Remember that I shall count on seeing you and as many of your family as you can persuade to come with you down in Washington some time in January."[15]

Such an invitation only added to Sewall's celebrity in northern Maine. Samuel Crabtree, the Island Falls correspondent to the *Bangor Daily News*, noted: "Bill Sewall, who figured so conspicuously at the Bangor state fair last week . . . greatly enjoyed his short visit with the President, and the genuine pleasure it gave him to meet his staunch friend of former days. His townspeople here naturally feel a pride in having one of their humble citizens thus honored by the nation's chief executive, and to no one would they rather see such an honor come, than to Bill Sewall—every honest man's friend."[16]

To go calling at the White House takes more than a little preparation, especially if you live in the backwoods. Mary and her fashion-conscious, eighteen-year-old daughter Kittie were concerned about what to wear. Not wanting to seem like hayseeds in the high society of Washington, they eagerly scanned Kittie's fashion magazines. Bill suggested that Mary hire the local seamstress to make a few dresses for the two women in the latest styles. Brothers Dave and Sam Sewall, "being very old, could not go,"[17] Bill recalled. His son, Fred, then a teen, would also accompany them. The Sewalls also had to make sure there was enough in the larder to provide for everyone else at the Sewall House while their friend Mrs. Bradford looked after the place in their absence.

In February 1903, they finally boarded the train and sped south through the cold countryside. With all of the preparations concluded, Mary finally relaxed and enjoyed herself, and Bill told her she'd never looked finer.[18] Roosevelt had arranged for Frank Hall, one of his assistants, to meet the Sewalls and take them to their room, Number 61 at the Oxford Hotel, and afterward to bring them to the White House. When they finally arrived at the executive mansion, the president was out riding, and they were told to make themselves comfortable.

After a time they heard footsteps coming down the hall—unmistakably the same fleet feet they remembered from Elkhorn. And then he was there, still dressed in his riding clothes. The president gave them a personal tour of the White House and afterward asked, "How do you like it, Bill?"

To which Sewall replied, "Why, it looks to me as how you've got a pretty good camp."

"It's always a good thing to have a good camp," Roosevelt concurred.[19]

Bill and TR spent much time talking during the visit, and both Sewalls enjoyed spending time with some of the newer Roosevelts, whom they'd only read about. The three younger members of the Sewall party—Kittie, Fred, and Wilmot Dow, Jr.—were secretly impressed by it all but they affected the teenage air of indifference. Mary later recalled that over the course of their stay in Washington the young people "delighted each other with their impersonations of the belles and beaux they saw."[20]

The congressional reception was held in the great East Room, and hundreds of invited guests were present. Mary "never saw anything so packed,"[21] and Bill squirmed in his fancy formal wear. As one reporter put it, "Mr. Sewall was in a frock coat and hardly knew what to do with himself." When they finally had a few minutes with the President, he asked them to join him behind the receiving ropes as a "mark of special favor."

The reception was followed with a dinner, during which Roosevelt turned to Sewall, put his hand affectionately on his shoulder, and asked him how he liked it all.

"Well," said Sewall, "I'm mighty glad to have come and seen it, and it'll give me something to talk about for all the rest of my life; but I'd rather go fishing for a steady thing."

The president laughed heartily, then in a semiconfidential whisper said, "So would I; but for goodness sake don't say it."[22]

Sewall did say it again—to a *New York Times* reporter. The reception "was my first and I guess it'll be my last. Can't say that I'd like to go very often. I'd rather go fishing and hunting, but it gives you a mighty fine chance to see the people—especially the women."[23]

The next several days were a whirlwind. The Sewalls toured many of the sights of the Washington area, from the Treasury Building to the Washington Monument to Mount Vernon, and sat in on a session of Congress. Sewall watched the proceedings for an hour or more from the president's seat, attracting a lot of attention. The party was joined by Senator Eugene Hale, a Republican from Turner, Maine, who sat behind Sewall and spent forty-five minutes pointing out the personalities below and explaining the goings-on. After they left, Roosevelt's close friend Senator Henry Cabot Lodge escorted the party around the Capitol.

Another afternoon, they sat for lunch with the President, and Roosevelt seated Mary to his left and Lizzie Dow to his right. Mary's nerves were jangling, because these were not supposed to be the seating arrangements. Secretary of State Elihu Root was supposed to be sitting next to Roosevelt but "did not understand he was invited,"[24] so Mary was moved closer to the President. She wrote home to Harriet that she "got through lunch fine." In fact, the family got through the entire week in good order. As Bill would say later, "I guess we had as fine a time as anybody that ever came to Washington."[25]

Besides the reunion of old friends, another interesting connection took place during the visit: the teenage sons of Sewall and Dow became fast friends with the teenage sons of the president. As a result, Kermit and Theodore, Jr., wanted badly to travel up to the Maine woods to go hunting with Fred and Wilmot, the Badlands babies. "In response to much urging, their father finally promised that they should go to Maine this year to hunt deer," reported the *New York Times* in a February 23 story.[26]

The press had an unending curiosity about this backwoods family, and a whole raft of articles were published on the visit. The February 7, 1903, *Boston Globe* ran a piece under the headline "Bill Sewall" that read, in part, "Bill Sewall of Maine, and there is only one Bill Sewall, the President's guide and mentor in his youth when he hunted and fished in the wilds of Maine, and later his ranchman in South Dakota, is in Washington today."[27]

But the newspapers seemed to want to play the story mostly for laughs. They accentuated the prince-and-the-pauper irony of the relationship, and the Sewalls were portrayed as rather comical, if not ridiculous, rustics. Roosevelt, of course, didn't see them this way.

Reported the *Boston Globe*: "There seemed to be a general surprise on the part of the public that the President should bestow so much attention on his old guide and his friends; but it was no surprise to the Sewalls, who know the kind of stuff Mr. Roosevelt is made of."

"I hadn't seen Theodore for sixteen years until last fall at Bangor," Sewall told the reporters who met him at Boston's South Station when his train pulled in at 3 p.m., "and he was the same Theodore then that he was in the Maine woods, when, more than thirty years ago, I used to guide him; the same that he was in the West when ranching, and the same that he is today. He doesn't forget his friends. He is not the kind likely to have his head turned by success."[28] Indeed, Roosevelt would say of the visit, "Never were there more welcome guests at the White House."[29]

The public may simply have been curious about the Sewalls but the newsmen had other ideas. "The newspapers could not resist caricaturing the guide whom the President entertained. William was at first less indignant than Mary, Kittie, and Fred, who felt it was most unfair."[30] By the time they reached home, though, even Sewall himself was furious. The aw-shucks portrayal of him and his family had become incessant, following them from Washington, D.C., to New York to Boston.

One of these pieces first appeared in the *New York Herald* on February 25, 1903 and was picked up by several other papers. It delighted in the fact that the Sewall party, all seven of them, were impressed by the tall buildings and subways of New York: "'Ground must be mighty dear,' observed 'Bill' sagely. 'I s'pose it comes at dollars to the foot about here. Kinder wish I didn't have to get back so soon. Like to stay a while, but got to get back home to Highland Falls. All tuckered out from our visit, ye see." Sewall's name —"Bill"— is in quotations for the entire 775 words and it's repeated for effect, sometimes three or four times per paragraph. The Mainer is quoted extensively, with lots of hillbillyish dialect, and the writer was too busy mocking the man even to get the name of his hometown right.

For his part, Sewall often played along, cracking wise. One reporter in New York noted that the huge holes being excavated for the subway "called for much wonder, which did not diminish much when it was explained that they were to be covered up and trains were to run in them at fifty miles an hour. 'Not for me,' remarked 'Bill' sententiously. 'I'm in no hurry to get underground till my time comes.'"[31]

The party made a grand tour of sorts on their way home. They visited friends and former Island Falls residents in Boston and Bill's cousins in Somerville, Massachusetts, and saw as many sights as they could fit into a few weeks' time—the Boston Public Library, the dry goods stores, Plymouth, and one of the largest ocean liners of the day, the *New England*. And the press followed them everywhere.

All this publicity—flattering or not—effectively launched Bill Sewall, the brand. He would be transformed into a celebrity, undoubtedly the most famous Maine guide and perhaps the most famous guide anywhere: "William Wingate Sewall, known all over the country as 'Bill Sewall' friend and hunting companion of President Roosevelt," as the *Boston Globe* put it in February 1903. Sewall became news fit to print—he was the subject of dozens of pieces in such papers as the *New York Times*, the *Washington Post*, the *Boston Globe*, the *Hartford Courant*, the *Portsmouth Herald*, and the *Atlanta Journal-Constitution*, and also was featured in *Harper's Monthly* and *The American* magazines.

The guide's new public profile led a lot of people to his door for hunting trips and more. He was asked to lend his name to certain products and to model for advertisements. A 1904 newspaper ad had Sewall wearing a broad-brimmed hat and full white beard standing proudly underneath the big bold letters of his name. It read: "President Roosevelt's Famous Maine Guide knows how to dress for cold weather; he wears the Sprague Russian Vest."[32] A Major General H. C. Merriam, of Prout's Neck, Maine, inquired in September 1907 whether Sewall would endorse a pack he made. "It is found to be a desirable help," he wrote. "I should like to know what you or others think of it."[33] Another magazine ran a clip on the "Guide's Paddle," designed by Bill Sewall.

Writers from all over the country would make the pilgrimage to Island Falls to interview the "Czar of Aroostook County" on a variety of issues relating to Roosevelt. In February 1906, the *New York Times* thought it noteworthy that Sewall was strapping himself in the latest fineries for another trip to Washington. The headline of the story read: "Sewall Gets a Frock Coat," and it simply noted that "for the first time in his life the big game hunter and sleuth of the forest will wear a frock coat, high collar, and silk hat." It was customary dress for society weddings in Washington, and he was on his way to attend the nuptials of TR's outspoken daughter Alice to Nicholas Longworth, congressman from Ohio. The magnificent White House ceremony would become arguably the wedding of the century. When Sewall left Island Falls, "an enthusiastic contingent of his fellow-citizens accompanied him and gave him three parting cheers as the train rolled out of the station."[34]

Just a couple of months before that, the *Boston Globe* had run a piece it picked up from the local *Machias Union*, about a visit Maine humorist S.A.D. Smith paid to the Sewall House. It amounted to little more than the quoted conversation between the two as they yarned away. Titled "Meddybemps' Philosophy," it opened with Smith quipping, "I am spending Sunday in Island Falls. It's the only thing you can spend here today because even the barber shop is closed."[35] They chatted quite a bit about TR and Sewall, and about Sewall and TR. And they brought up the touchy subject of Sewall's new post—Collector of Customs for Aroostook County.

Czar of Aroostook County

A few days after returning from his 1903 visit to the White House, Bill Sewall was back cutting trees. He may have become famous, but he still rose early and worked to make something of each day. He still cut wood in the winter, farmed in the summer, and served as sheriff year-round.

Now that TR was president, the guide had a new hobby—Sewall began studying his friend's career in earnest, reading everything he could about his administration. The bedroom TR had stayed in on the third floor of the Sewall House became a little shrine to the twenty-sixth president, packed with books and clippings and photographs. As the election of 1904 neared, Bill could "think of little else," his wife would later recall, and she was rather astonished at his concern. Mary's biographer recounted one conversation where Mary tried to reassure her husband by pointing out that the newspapers and public opinion both indicated that Roosevelt would win.

"Mary, you can't be sure," was his reply. "Nobody ever knows for sure who will win an election until it's over. Strong leaders make enemies and the public is fickle. Some rumor might rob him of votes enough to defeat him. I've never wanted to see women voting, but this time I wish they were. Women are more concerned with right and wrong, and he'd win for sure if they voted."[1]

He needn't have worried. Roosevelt handily beat challenger Alton Brooks Parker, carrying thirty-two states, including Maine and both Dakotas, to the Democrat's thirteen, much to the relief of most everyone in Island Falls.

Not long after the election, the Sewalls received another invitation from the White House, this time for the inauguration in March. And again the coveted invite was for as many Sewalls as wanted to come. Bill had been waiting for this day, eager to see his friend sworn into office by popular vote rather than having been "shot in." He and Mary were thrilled, but as ever there was much to do.

For one thing, their daughter Kittie was engaged, and she very much wanted her fiancé, Tom Tracey, to attend the inauguration with her—which meant that, before they traveled to Washington to watch Roosevelt take the oath of office, they'd first have to take their own vows. The wedding took place on a blustery day in early March 1905, the day before the family was to leave for Washington. Kittie was married in the parlor of the Sewall House, just as her parents had been had so many years before.

Everything went as planned, and a huge entourage of Sewalls boarded the train for Washington the next day. Traveling with Bill and Mary this time were Fred, Harriett, Nancy; Kittie and her new husband; and Miss Luvie Hackett, a schoolteacher who was boarding with the Sewalls. "William had never been so happy,"[2] recalled Mary.

On this trip, they were guests in the home of a White House guard. The Sewalls would never forget the spectacle of the March 4 inauguration: the military bands, the six Native American chiefs, the Rough Riders, the flowers, and the cheering crowds. During the ceremony, they were seated so near the president that Fred said he easily could have reached out and touched him.

After the inauguration they lunched with several Roosevelt family members and distinguished friends, including Bamie, Corinne, Uncle Robert Roosevelt, social reformer Jacob Riis, and noted New York architect Grant La Farge and his wife, Florence. That evening they attended the president's gala banquet and enjoyed the "sumptuous menu prepared by foreign chefs."[3]

They didn't get to see quite as much of TR as on their first trip to Washington, but they still had time to catch up. Roosevelt would later remark that on these visits to the White House, "we talked over everything, public and private, past and present; the education and future careers of our children, the proper attitude of the United States in external and internal matters. We all of us looked at the really important matters of public policy and private conduct from substantially the same viewpoint."[4]

When the Sewall party went to the theater, they sat in the president's box, and even without the president being present, all eyes were on them once again. Bill recalled: "When we seemed to attract a good deal of attention. . . . I told the ladies, who were rather bothered by it, that it was perfectly natural, the people had found something green from the country."[5]

After his treatment by the press on his previous visit, Sewall was wise enough to avoid reporters and keep his mouth shut this time, and all in all the family had a superb time.

Bill Sewall had known before the inauguration that T.H. Phair, of Presque Isle, was retiring as customs collector for the District of Aroostook. Based in Houlton, this was a plum position, with a staff of thirteen deputies and a salary of about three thousand dollars, and Bill Sewall was keen to hold it.[6] And he was an attractive candidate. The job entailed a variety of responsibilities, from collecting duties on imported goods to catching smugglers who attempted to move contraband across the border. Already widely respected as a sheriff's deputy, a vaunted guide, and a prominent Aroostook businessman, Sewall didn't surprise anyone when he decided to campaign for the job. The position required a federal appointment, and the guide knew just whom to turn to for assistance in landing it. He didn't hesitate—and neither did the president.

Upon writing to Roosevelt for help, Sewall got a note back. "I shall see Congressman Powers and Senator Hale just as soon as they get back here," TR responded. "I shall try my best to arrange it." True to his word, in December 1905, Roosevelt wrote to the ranking congressman who oversaw customs matters:

> I am going to ask you not to object to my sending the name of William W. Sewall for the Collector of Customs for the District of Aroostook, Maine. I think that you will agree with me that Mr. Sewall is entirely competent. Under ordinary circumstances I should follow your preference in the matter; but this is a peculiar case, for Sewall is an old friend of mine whom I have known for nearly thirty years, with whom I have lived and hunted both in the fall and in the winter in Maine, and with whom I have lived and worked year in and year out on a ranch on the Little Missouri. You know the peculiar ties that bind one to a man in whose company one has known toil and hardship, hunger and cold, and with whom one has fronted risks and overcome difficulties. I can personally guarantee Bill Sewall's courage, honesty, and efficiency, and I hope you will agree to his appointment."[7]

The *Boston Daily Globe* looked on with interest, calling the race between the guide and his opponent, Houlton lawyer Ransford Shaw, "one of the most picturesque and interesting political canvasses ever known in Maine." Shaw had expected to cruise into the position, and while eminently qualified, Sewall nonetheless came into the race as a "rank outsider as far as the political machine went." According to the newspaper account, Sewall and his opponent were attempting to succeed "one of the most prominent and wealthy men of Aroostook, known as the 'Starch King,'" and Phair himself "was not at all averse to renomination."

Having a popular president in his corner was a huge asset for Sewall, but he knew he couldn't ask for Roosevelt's help unless he put in the work himself, actively campaigning. He started out a year ahead of time, walking the district, "on foot and alone, as he had tracked down a bull moose many a time." Sewall explained to the *Boston Globe* reporter that "although he was a friend of the President's he wanted to show Mr. Roosevelt how he stood with the people." The people loved him. "His success was instantaneous," continued the *Globe* story.

"When he was all through he had yards and yards of petitions signed by some of the best people of the county. He had secured a backing which would have demanded recognition had the President never heard of him."

"'Bill' Sewall is considered a man of intelligence, education, unquestioned integrity and good judgment," the Beantown reporter gushed, "and amply qualified to tackle all the problems that may arise in the administration of the Custom House."[8] Sewall lived up to his billing, serving as customs collector for a decade and winning reappointment by a president who was *not* a close personal friend, William Howard Taft. He commuted from Island Falls to Houlton on the train line that he had helped bring to his hometown, and, once arrived in Houlton, he could always count on being offered a ride to his office.

Running the customs service in Aroostook County in 1905 was not without its dangers. The North Woods border between the United States and Canada was a porous one, and smuggling was common. "Rum" (the term Mainers used for all booze) was continually on the move between the nations, and even produce such as potatoes was surreptitiously shipped from New Brunswick to Maine, where they fetched twenty-five cents more a bushel. (Wool was another commodity that sold for considerably more in the States—as much as twelve cents a pound more. Eggs went for five cents more a dozen.)[9]

Despite all this trafficking, and the fact that an Aroostook deputy had once almost been run down by a stage and was subsequently whipped, Bill Sewall refused to wear a sidearm. Mary once overheard him talking to their son Fred about it: "I don't intend to carry a gun. I've gotten along in a lot of rough company without it up to now." The other men in the office did carry weapons, but they could never persuade the old sheriff. The lifelong hunter, perhaps recalling his days in the Badlands, always felt that guns heightened the tension in confrontations and that they "made the other man uneasy and could lead to trouble."[10]

Somehow Sewall found the stamina to do it all—customs collector, sheriff, guide, logger, farmer, hotelier. Mary Sewall used to marvel at her husband's energy: "The little sleeping he did always amazed."[11] And there was more. In 1903, Bill had purchased a mile-square lot on Hook Point, a woodsy peninsula in Mattawamkeag Lake. The parcel curved like a flexing bicep around West Cove, and it was the highest point on the ten-mile-long lake, with a sweeping view of the lower half of Mattawamkeag. On the lot were two established sporting enterprises—Bradford Camp and the Berry Boy's Camp—which Sewall incorporated into his new business, called Hook Point Camps.

Sewall House would be closed for the summers, while the whole Sewall family was employed at Hook Point Camps. Mary and the girls did the laundry. The boys guided for Bill and did repair work with him. Bill's siblings visited often—his brother Sam and niece Pauline were among the first guests—and could be counted on to lend still more hands.

Success came quickly. In his first month, Sewall hosted sports from Portland, Pittsfield, Bucksport, Bar Harbor, Oakfield, and Houlton, Maine; Boston, Amesbury, and South Framingham, Massachusetts; and Philadelphia. By 1907, more than two hundred names were recorded in the guest registry. Many guests came, of course, to meet and travel with Maine's most famous guide. As Sewall had foreseen, "the camps attracted numerous people including fishermen and hunters, members of the Roosevelt family and their friends, people who had read about William in the metropolitan papers or magazines. . . . Many returned again and again."[12]

Thanks to the coming of rail, the boosterism of guides like Cornelia "Flyrod" Crosby, who worked the outdoor expositions of New York, and magazines such as the Bangor and Aroostook's *In the Maine Woods*, the North Woods were enjoying boom times as a destination, and Island Falls was no exception. The local *Bangor Daily News* correspondent reported that in 1904 more sportsmen were coming to the Mattawamkeag hamlet than ever before: "The facilities are as good as can be found anywhere and the sportsmen are beginning to appreciate the fact."[13]

The Sewalls' camp was among the finest in the area, and its appeal extended far beyond hunters and fishermen. People came to northern Maine to escape the heat of the cities and relax among the pines, just as the Roosevelts had done. They swam, motored or paddled the lake, climbed area peaks, hiked in to Bible Point, and enjoyed evenings around the bonfire. There were taffy pulls when the weather was optimal (low humidity was required). Mary's homemade ice cream was a favorite on Sundays, and the younger girls often made fudge.

Bill and Mary would typically stay five months on the lake, and thanks to the presence of numerous Sewalls, their friends, and other regulars, the place had the feel of an ongoing family reunion. When Harriet and her husband, George, or Fred and his friends came by, the hosts would automatically become "Aunt Mary and Uncle William" to everyone staying there.[14]

Busy as he was, Sewall always took time to read the morning newspaper to keep up with Roosevelt's career, and his favorable impression of his friend never wavered. "William followed Theodore's presidency from day to day,"[15] Mary later recalled. The pair continued their correspondence, and Sewall would write TR telling how proud he was of him and how much he admired the work he was doing.

Even as president, TR was happy to hear he still pleased his old guide. "I am mighty glad you like what I have been doing in the governmental field," he wrote to Sewall in 1906. "I do not have to tell you that my great hero is Abraham Lincoln and I have wanted while President to be the same representative of the plain people; in the same sense that he was; not of course with the same genius and power that he had but according to my lights, along the same lines."[16] A couple of years later he said much the same: "While I have been President I have tried to make the plain people feel that I was especially their representative and have their interests close at heart, and if I have succeeded I am more than pleased."[17]

By 1909 Theodore Roosevelt's achievements in office were undeniable, from the construction of the Panama Canal to the conservation of the nation's national resources—an issue that resonated deeply with Sewall. TR came to conservation via his passion for hunting, and Sewall, of course, was his greatest hunting mentor. The picture Roosevelt drew of a good game warden, something he thought the Adirondacks needed when he was serving as governor in Albany, bears a resemblance to a certain Island Falls man: "I want as game protectors men of courage, resolution, and hardihood, who can handle the rifle, ax, and paddle; who can camp out in summer and winter; who can go on snowshoes, if necessary; who can go through the woods by day or by night with out regard to trails."[18]

He held outdoorsmen in the highest esteem and equated them with patriots. "Hardy outdoor sports, like hunting, are in themselves of no small value to the national character and should be encouraged in every way," he wrote in his autobiography, adding that "men who go into the wilderness, indeed, men who take part in any field sports with horse and rifle, receive a benefit which can hardly be given by even the most vigorous athletic games."[19]

In *Hero Tales from American History*, a 1919 book that TR coauthored with Henry Cabot Lodge, he wrote about pioneers and men who made their names in the woods. While Lodge profiled George Washington, Abraham Lincoln, and John Quincy Adams, Roosevelt extolled the manly accomplishments of Daniel Boone, George Rogers Clarke, Davy Crockett, Sam Houston, and the backwoodsmen of Kings Mountain, on the border between North and South Carolina.

By the early twentieth century, America's forest lands—spiritual home of these men, as well as Sewall and, to a certain extent, Roosevelt himself—were in jeopardy. TR felt it keenly. As Mary Sewall put it, he feared "the natural wealth of the nation was disappearing at an alarming rate."[20] Half of the timberlands that had covered the nation when it was first settled had been hewed down. The great herds of buffalo that once stampeded from North Carolina to Alaska fell just as certainly as the trees and were now facing extinction; many other animals were in line to follow. Roosevelt knew this personally, having gone west to hunt bison before they were gone and being the last "trained" witness to see a passenger pigeon.[21] Developers were eying pristine tracts of wildlands, and the rate of destruction seemed to be intensifying exponentially.

As president, TR said as much at the first conference of governors, which he convened in 1908 to study the nation's conservation issues: "In the development, the use, and therefore the exhaustion of certain of the natural resources, the progress has been more rapid in the past century and a quarter than during all preceding time of which we have record."[22]

Roosevelt had begun to combat that trend back when he became governor of New York. He tightened loose game laws, giving the Fisheries, Forestry, and Game Commission some much needed muscle, helped to create the Palisades Interstate Park, and recommended that the Adirondacks and the Catskills be made into "great parks kept in perpetuity for the benefit and enjoyment of our people."[23]

When he ascended to the White House, he kept conservation at the top of his agenda. "The first work I took up when I became President was the work of reclamation," he declared in his autobiography. And indeed his first message to Congress on December 3, 1901, included a speech about the importance of natural resources. "The forest and the water problems," he asserted, "are perhaps the most vital internal problems of the United States."[24]

In a 1907 speech at the Deep Waterway Convention in Memphis, he repeated this conviction: "The conservation of natural resources is the fundamental problem. Unless we solve that problem it will avail us little to solve all the others."[25]

To that end, Roosevelt created the Bureau of Forestry in 1907. In 1908 he convened the governors for a congress on natural resources, and the result of the meeting was that these chief executives returned home and—thirty-six of them at least—started their own state conservation commissions. At the federal level a national Conservation Commission was launched on June 8, 1908 and tasked with taking an inventory of all of the natural resources in each state. The President called the final report of the commission, which was presented to Congress, "one of the most fundamentally important documents ever laid before the American people."[26]

During his tenure, Roosevelt worked tirelessly at protecting the nation's natural heritage, saving some 84,000 acres a day. He was actively involved in the creation of 150 national forests, 5 national parks, 4 national game preserves, 18 national monuments (including the Grand Canyon), 24 reclamation projects, and 51 federal bird reserves (including the first, on Pelican Island, Florida).[27]

Not only did he protect these wild places, he reveled in them in a way no previous president had, becoming "increasingly dependent on the friendship of nature for relief from the cares of office."[28] He made grand trips—hiking in Yosemite with John Muir, for example—and simpler ones—walking regularly in Washington's Rock Creek Park, often inviting foreign dignitaries to join him.

Roosevelt knew that conservation would be his legacy, and he was immensely proud of what he'd done. "During the seven and a half years closing on March 4,

1909," he wrote in his autobiography, "more was accomplished for the protection of wildlife in the United States than during all the previous years, excepting only the creation of Yellowstone National Park."[29]

When Theodore Roosevelt took office in 1904 he had stated emphatically that he wouldn't seek a third term. There were a variety of reasons for this resolve, not the least of which was the pressure the office put on his family. Also, as he told Bill Sewall in a letter in June of 1908, it was "for the very reason that I believe in being a strong President and making the most of the office and using it without regard to the little, feeble, snarling men who yell about executive usurpation, I also believe it is not a good thing that any one man should hold it too long. My ambition is, in however humble a manner and however far off, to travel in the footsteps of Washington and Lincoln."[30]

Sewall thought he made good on this aspiration, that he did travel in those footsteps, and what pleased him the most was that his friend also "put into practice the principles he had expressed when he was a boy in Maine and when he was a young man in Dakota. It just seemed to me that he was giving public expression to what I had always known was in him."[31] But the guide also felt that TR's very strength in office was what should have compelled him to continue leading the country. When Sewall received an invitation to Taft's inauguration, he decided to go largely because he wanted to hear from Roosevelt himself why TR thought Taft would be better for the nation.[32]

By the end of TR's presidency, though, Bill Sewall got the feeling the office was losing its luster for Roosevelt. A *Boston Globe* reporter made the trek to Island Falls one day in July in 1908 to grill the guide about his friend and found him busy keeping one eye on a forest fire that he thought might stray too close to Island Falls. Sewall was also a little press-shy by this time—"as always, he was willing to talk about the President, although with due caution," the reporter noted.

When the writer wondered whether he still got letters from Roosevelt, Sewall allowed as how he did. The logical follow up question: What was on the president's mind? Sewall mentioned that TR had expressed concern about his weight, adding that he could offer the perfect solution: "Guess if he'd come down here he could take a little of it off helping me to my hay, and I reckon he'd do more work than any two of my hired men."

The guide went on to say the president seemed to have a stronger desire than ever to return to Mattawamkeag. "I think that he's glad that his job at the White House is most over," Sewall told the reporter. "He tells me he's hankerin' to smell the pines of old Maine once more, and he's the same as promised me to come down to my camps for a spell after election and practice a little on deer and moose round here before he goes to Africa to hunt lions and tigers. I know well enough that he'll come and bring some of the boys."[33]

But TR never did.

Instead, Sewall journeyed yet again to Washington—this time by himself—to see Roosevelt. The guide was one of thousands from all over the country who came to pay their respects as the twenty-sixth president left office. The crowds were enormous. "The last days of Mr. Roosevelt in the White House are crowded more than those of any of his predecessors," observed the *New York Times*. "Swarms of people [came] to Washington, many of them from considerable distances, merely to pass in line by the President at his usual informal noonday reception and shake hands with him and say good-bye."[34]

The president's intimates were invited for a last supper of sorts. Sewall dined with a host of TR's friends as a de facto member of his famous "Tennis Cabinet." These were those colleagues and confidantes with whom the president surrounded himself during his walks in Rock Creek Park, his hunting trips, and his tennis hours. Thirty-one of them gathered for one final meal, including all manner of dignitaries, from Supreme Court Justice William Henry Moody to the French Ambassador, Jules Jusserand. Beside these refined men of state was a cast of characters with whom Sewall likely felt at home: forest service commissioner and staunch Roosevelt ally Gifford Pinchot, Oklahoma Rough Rider Jack Abernathy, frontier marshal Seth Bullock, and another of the president's old guides, Indian fighter "Yellowstone" Kelly.

Roosevelt lauded the men for their service to him and their country, said that they represented the best kinds of Americans, and credited his successes in office to them. They, in turn, presented him with a plaque engraved with a crouching cougar.

The president's words were poignant and in many ways seemed aimed right at his friend from Island Falls: "Whether a man is a cabinet Minister, a bureau chief, a Marshal, an Indian agent, a forester, a letter carrier, a member of the Life-Saving Service, a clerk in a department, or a workman in a navy yard, or whether he holds one of a hundred other positions, makes not the slightest difference if he puts his heart and soul and his mind into his work, and is content to accept as his chief reward the satisfaction that comes from knowledge that the work has been well done.

"So, while I greet you for yourselves, I greet you still more as symbolizing others. . . ."[35]

The Passing of a Grand Old Man

In December of 1911, Bill Sewall got another note from Roosevelt. The fifty-three-year-old former president was thinking about another climb up Maine's highest peak. "I tell you I should hate to try to follow 'Old Bill Sewall' up Katahdin," he confessed. "Indeed I should hate to go up Katahdin at all, no matter how slowly, unless I had a month in the Maine woods first to try to get back into some condition."[1]

The idea of a rendezvous in Island Falls still captivated TR. He didn't make it that far north, but he did put in an appearance in Maine a few months later, speaking in Portland in March of 1912, during his final campaign for president. He'd decided Taft had made enough of a mess of things in just four years, and once again he wanted to be the nominee of the Republican Party.

Bill Sewall was in Portland with "fully 4,000" others to greet him. "I think I agreed with pretty near everything he did," the guide recalled, "and when he came out for the Republican nomination in the spring of 1912 I was with him with all the strength I possessed."[2] Like Roosevelt, he later switched from the Republicans to the Bull Moose Party.

The event made headlines because just before Roosevelt was to give his speech, the stage collapsed underneath him. "The Colonel was thrown heavily," read the *New York Times* account, "but he didn't for a moment lose his nerve." When he regained his footing, Roosevelt threw his arms up to indicate he was unhurt. The audience proceeded to applaud him for "fully three minutes," during which time the former chief executive cooked up a quip: "It was the weight of intellect that caused the platform to break down, but it was not our platform. Our platform won't break down."

Again, he recognized Sewall publicly, calling out, "Well, Bill Sewall, how are you?" and then explaining to the crowd that the two went back decades together.[3]

His platform may not have broken but it did lose—disastrously. The Republicans renominated Taft in June, Roosevelt was forced to run under the banner of the progressive Bull Moose party, and the election went to the Democratic candidate, Woodrow Wilson. The result sent TR into a funk, and in 1913 he once again retreated to the wilds, this time to the Amazon rainforest, a region as yet unmapped and, for a lifelong naturalist, full of uncatalogued delights. His son Kermit was accompanying him, and he wanted Sewall to come along, too: "By George! I wish you were going on that South American trip. We won't do much hunting, but it will be interesting in some ways."[4]

Deep in the Brazilian rainforest, TR found himself thinking once again of his adventures in Aroostook County. On one of the long carries, necessitated by rapids deemed too fast to paddle, he "longed for a big Maine birchbark, such as that in which I once went down the Mattawamkeag at high water! It would have slipped down these rapids as a girl trips through a country-dance."[5]

Roosevelt's fateful trip down the River of Doubt, his "last chance to be a boy!"[6] turned into a deep and dark expedition to the brink of madness. He injured his leg and contracted malaria, and at one point actually contemplated suicide to spare his crew the hardship of carrying him through the jungle. He lost one of his best men to the river, and another member of his team came unhinged and killed his sergeant. Rather than being a glorious adventure during which the weary campaigner could bond with his son and regroup from his defeats, the 1,000-mile trek was the beginning of the end.

There was no fanfare to greet Roosevelt on his return, and the darkness he'd encountered in the rainforest seemed to follow him. He came back "thinner and older looking," according to the *New York Times*, and he walked with a cane and referred to himself as an "old man."[7]

His friend up north didn't care. Bill wanted to visit New York, telling his wife, "how much he would like to see Theodore and hear him tell of his experience."[8]

The pair would see each other one last time, but it was in Maine, not New York. Roosevelt had a speaking engagement in Portland in March 1918, and he wrote Sewall excitedly: "Friend William, You can bet I will see you if I don't see another human being when I am at Portland! Present this letter so that you may have immediate admission to me wherever I am. I don't know as yet at what hotel they will put me up."[9]

And Sewall was there, the first person to greet Roosevelt as he stepped off the train in Portland on March 28. The former president was in town to address the Republican state convention, his first public speech since his Amazon fiasco. The war in Europe was much on his mind. He felt it was mismanaged and that an injection of five million men from the United States was needed.

As usual, Roosevelt was prepared to put his battered body where his mouth was. Age and injury didn't prevent him, at fifty-nine, from publicly offering to form a division, much as he'd done with the Rough Riders, to "beat down Germany."[10] TR offered President Wilson his services—he'd build a small army and command it himself. Bill Sewall was as astonished as TR when Wilson waved the offer aside, telling Roosevelt he had a desk full of letters from would-be volunteers, but that he would be using the draft and the regular army instead. For TR, it was "undoubtedly the keenest disappointment of his life,"[11] and it sent him into another period of melancholy.

Much of the rest of his family, however, did serve in the Great War. All four sons enlisted, and his daughter Ethel was a Red Cross nurse in Paris. And his sons would fall: Archie was wounded, and Quentin, a pilot, was killed just four months after TR spoke in Portland. This was a blow that was almost physically felt by Roosevelt, and he never really recovered from it. Now he had heartsickness to go with the physical difficulties he'd been suffering from since his Brazilian odyssey.

Even from Island Falls, Sewall could tell his friend was in bad shape, and he mused with friends and family about the natural, political, and human forces that had conspired against Theodore. Even so, Sewall felt that TR would get back on his feet, that his "vigor would return," and the nation would see its mistake and turn to the former president once again for leadership.[12]

Roosevelt also seemed to recognize that he was failing. He wrote to Sewall, "I'm not what I used to be, Will. I'm fast becoming a worn old man. But you, old friend, will never grow old. You will be young always."[13]

Bill Sewall had seen it coming, as he had with so many other things between them. Even so, he found himself in disbelief—Roosevelt was only sixty, in the prime of his life, and the guide could never stop thinking of him as the vigorous young man he remembered from that hilltop in the Dakota Territory. And now the lion was dead.

"His sudden death was no surprise to me," the guide would later acknowledge. "For I know that he had many weak spells when he suffered from heart trouble." The same troubles that they'd laughed about so many years ago, when Roosevelt was defying his Harvard doctor's orders by climbing the mountains of Mount Desert, had caught up with him.

TR had kept his condition a secret from most people, just as his father had. "The only way one could tell it was his unusual silence for two or three days at a time," Sewall would say. "I doubt whether his immediate family always knew that he was suffering."[14] For several months, Roosevelt had been in and out of hospitals for issues related to the leg he'd injured in Brazil and rheumatism so bad he couldn't walk. One spell required seven weeks' recuperation, and his physician told him he might never walk again.

He did walk again, and he worked continuously on writing projects, and was asked to run again for governor of New York, an offer he declined. Some thought he might seek the nomination for president again in the 1920 election, but he had no interest in that either.

Ten months after the Portland visit, on January 5, 1919, he complained of trouble breathing. His doctor was summoned and prescribed a sleeping aid. TR went off to bed that night never to wake again. A coronary embolism took him as he slept, extinguishing a force of nature.

With the passing of Roosevelt, a light seemed to go out in Bill Sewall. At seventy-four he was still running the occasional river drive and would continue at it for another year. (He was given the honor of overseeing the last log drive on the Mattawamkeag in 1920.) He was still working at the camps every summer. But the death of his lifelong friend seemed to deliver the kind of blow to him that TR's Amazon trip had dealt to the former president. When Roosevelt died, Mary "felt as though one of their own had perished," as her biographer put it. And she couldn't help noticing the changes in her husband: "There was a stoop in his shoulders, a faraway look in his eyes as though he now lived in the past."[15]

For a while, Sewall couldn't sleep. To ease his mind, he wrote to TR's widow, Edith, and also expressed his condolences to each of Theodore's sons and daughters. Over and over he reread the letters Roosevelt had sent to Island Falls with all his promises to visit again.

Two months later Sewall received a letter from the Theodore Roosevelt Permanent Memorial National Committee. Inside was an invitation to join the organization, which had been set up to determine a fitting tribute to the fallen commander in chief. He was proud to be part of such an endeavor and accepted the invitation immediately. His work with the memorial association would give shape to the rest of his life.[16]

Bill Sewall traveled to New York in March of 1919 with his daughter Nancy, who was bothered by the fact that he insisted on traveling in his blue flannel shirt. He told her he was a woodsman and wanted people to know it.

She'd later remark that this trip was the first time she'd seen her father cry. One of the Sewalls' first stops was at Sagamore Hill, where Bill sadly walked through Roosevelt's old house, looking over all the tangibles of his friend's life. He strolled paths through the woods, visited the modest grave where his friend was interred—"A quiet place, close to nature, and away from the bustle of the world. That's just like the Colonel," he said. And he marveled at the number of birdhouses on the property, commenting that the "Colonel did love the birds."[17]

After the tour, reporters met him at the Hotel Commodore, and pestered him for details and reminiscences. Sewall told them, as the *New York Times* put it, that it would be "difficult to exhaust him of all the significant occurrences during his experiences with 'Theodore.'" Though it had long been the vogue to call Roosevelt "Teddy," his old friend still referred to him as Theodore. "Teddy," Sewall liked to say, was too small a name for such a great man.[18]

But the purpose of the trip was to help come up with an appropriate memorial to the man, and the committee met to gather ideas on March 24, 1919, chartering and renaming itself the Roosevelt Memorial Association. Sewall thought whatever they decided, the memorial should have some utility to it, and he spoke at length about why he felt this way: "He would have liked something in the way of an institution that would teach Americanism—that would put into men a sense of justice and truth. I know that no statue or monument would have pleased him. He would have wanted nothing that had no practical use."[19]

The association elected to follow three paths—locate an appropriate monument in Washington, D.C.; create a public park in Oyster Bay, New York; and raise the necessary funds to create a Theodore Roosevelt Association that would disseminate the ideas of "Great-Heart" to the nation. Each goal was accomplished over time. The park at Oyster Bay opened in 1928. Theodore Roosevelt Island, a ninety-one-acre isle in the Potomac, was purchased in 1932, and Congress approved funds for a memorial there in 1960. And the Theodore Roosevelt Association continues to do its work to this day.

For his part, Sewall chose to honor his friend in his own way, which TR would no doubt have appreciated. When he was in New York, the old guide was invited to speak all across the city at fraternal organizations, women's clubs, and boys' schools, telling stories about Roosevelt and their many adventures together. Sewall was still recognized and treated as a celebrity. If Roosevelt was a great man, then the man who guided and mentored him must have been someone special, too.

One of these talks took him to the Roosevelt Military Academy in West Englewood, New Jersey, where someone suggested he open a summer camp on Mattawamkeag Lake, so that other boys could have experiences like those Theodore Roosevelt once had. Sewall was entranced with the idea and immediately began to consider the possibilities.

He was so well received at the academy, in fact, that he was repeatedly invited back to instruct the boys in woodcraft right there in New Jersey. He traveled down on several occasions in early 1921, and spent a month at the school, teaching astronomy, tracking, map and compass reading, and ax handling, which he demonstrated by driving a stake into the ground and proceeding to fell a tree atop it. The school's president called him "about the toughest piece of human timber of his age in the world," and waxed enthusiastically about the visit to a reporter from the *Houlton Times*: "A remarkable contrast was illustrated by this tall, raw-boned pioneer with his white beard, competing with youngsters of nine and ten years of age in stiff woods outings."[20]

Sewall had a fine time, writing home to Mary, "I am well, being as well used as if I belonged to the Royal Family." When he wasn't instructing the youngsters in the skills of the woods, he crossed into New York to meet up with friends. "I am trying to see everybody that I know," he said, "and have seen most of them—Mr. Emlen Roosevelt, Mrs. Douglas Robinson, Hagedorne [sic], Hanks, Mr. Akley. . . ."[21]

During a conversation with a reporter from the *New York Times*, Sewall put the lie to a common misconception about his friend, debunking a myth that TR's whole image had been built around. He thought it would be inspirational for boys like the ones at the academy to know the truth about Theodore Roosevelt, but it no doubt shocked a few hero-worshippers: "Most people have the idea that he was a strong man. He was far from that; he was physically weak all his life, but he never let it be known except to those with whom he was most intimate. The reason people did not know about it was that he never gave in. He was full of grit, and did not know how to complain."[22]

Mary Sewall always worried when her husband traveled, and the fact that he was now seventy-five only heightened her anxieties. When he returned from New York, after stopping to visit their daughter Harriet in Fitchburg, Massachusetts, she was relieved as ever. After they caught up with one another, though, she surprised him with a reprimand: "William, can't you ever learn to stay out of a scuffle?"

While in Fitchburg, Sewall had come to the aid of a policeman who was trying to arrest a man in front of crowd of onlookers that were goading and harassing him. Mary had gotten word from Harriet about the incident, and the couple had a good laugh about the Massachusetts police who couldn't make an arrest without the aid of an elderly Maine lawman.[23]

Although the old North Woods sheriff resumed work, Roosevelt was never far from his mind. He continued to be asked for comments, whether by the press or by organizations requesting an appearance. One such invitation came in August 1921, when the chairman of Good Will Farm for needy boys, in Hinckley, Maine, wrote him to inquire whether he would help dedicate a tablet to honor the twenty-sixth president at a new 1,000-acre section of trails at Good Will.

Sewall also busied himself with his memoirs. The same year that Roosevelt died, the guide published *Bill Sewall's Story of T.R.*, a short account of their adventures together. Most of its 116 pages focus on their time in the Badlands, a beautiful story of friendship and admiration, and you can almost see his tears in the final few pages: "He is dead now and all the world is seeing what I saw forty years ago, and saying about him what I said when we lived under the same roof in the Dakota days. I knew him well, for I saw him under all conditions. . . . It is no use for me to name his good qualities. It is enough for me to say that I think he had more than any man I have ever known and more than any man the world has produced since Lincoln."[24]

Sewall reiterated this sentiment almost word for word when a writer sent him a letter asking about TR's character. With a scratchy scrawl and characteristic bluntness, Sewall wrote back: "It is needless for me to attempt to name all his good qualities, since he is dead and the world appreciates them. He was one of the greatest men the world has ever produced."[25]

In February of 1922 the Aroostook man took a copy of the book he had written about his friend and presented it to a new shrine to Roosevelt, at his boyhood home at 28 East 20th Street, which had been turned into a museum and opened to the public by the sister organization of the Theodore Roosevelt Memorial Association.

The guide's own memorial and tribute was coming along nicely in the woods along the Mattawamkeag. Sewall knew just what it should be: "The kind of institution I mean would be a school to teach boys to be Americans along the lines that [Roosevelt's] own boys were taught, because there could be no better kind. Of course, there would be woodcraft and out-of-door sorts, and all that sort of thing. The boy would be taught to take care of himself, and to use other men as he ought to."[26]

In the summer of 1923, just such a camp opened, with thirty boys and six counselors—right at Hook Point. Sewall had retrofitted his largest building, Briggs Camp, to serve as the camp's lodge. Camp Roosevelt gave the guide a new focus—he was no longer sheriff or customs collector. Every year he and his sons prepared the facility, cut firewood, and lent whatever aid was needed during the weeks of camp. The campers would come by boat, paddling down the Mattawamkeag, just as TR had, and during the day Bill Sewall would teach them woodcraft, hunting, and fishing, much the way he had shown a young Harvard student so many years before.

Evenings at camp meant stories. Sewall would tell the boys of his time with the President, about meeting him as a teenager, of hunting and fishing with him right on those very waters, of their experiences out West, of Red Finnegan and the Gros Ventre Indians. How a sickly boy not much older than they were, by sheer determination, built himself into the kind of man who could be president.

Winters upcountry, though, were getting harder. For Sewall they had always meant long days in the woods cutting trees. Now in his eighties, he lacked the mobility for that sort of work and was relegated to whittling and puttering at home, and it was a constant source of frustration for a man who'd spent so much of his life outside. After a few years, Bill and Mary began spending the winters with their daughter Harriet and her family in Andover, New Hampshire. They relished the time with their grandchildren and enjoyed themselves in their new community, but it wasn't the same as being in Island Falls, and, just as they had on the Dakota plains, they spent most of their days dreaming of Aroostook County. During the winters of 1926, 1927, and 1928, as Mary's biographer put it, they "were living to return to Island Falls."[27]

Each summer they'd return, Bill telling Roosevelt stories and teaching the boys about the woods, Mary helping run Camp Roosevelt. The camp would continue at Hook Point through 1928, when it moved to nearby Pleasant Lake, a mile north of Mattawamkeag, where it ran as a camp for boys until 1932 when it became an adult camp.

Harriet and her family relocated to Raymond, New Hampshire, and Bill and Mary followed her there to spend the winter of 1930. Once settled into their small house, Bill came down with a cold. It was February, and the cold didn't seem unusual, but the old guide was now in his eighties, when any illness could be serious. It wasn't until the local doctor paid a visit and indicated that Sewall's prospects for recovery were not good that Mary realized the severity of the situation. Sewall fought as best he could, struggling on for weeks before succumbing on the morning of March 16, 1930.

A day later, the *Bangor Daily News* extolled Sewall as "one of the most famous residents of Aroostook," recalling the time decades earlier when he entertained "J. West Roosevelt, a New York physician, and W.E. Roosevelt, a New York banker, both cousins of the ex-President. They knew what they were talking about when they recommended the good graces of Mr. Sewall for an outing for young Teddy to build up his health. For three autumns and one winter Roosevelt hunted and trapped with Sewall. Those days in the pines, among the bears and deer, changed him from a delicate youth into a sturdy man, and the strength he gained up there was his making and served him well in his later years."[28]

An obituary in a local paper, a funeral service at the Whittier Congregational Church in Island Falls—there were no grand parades or memorial associations founded when Bill Sewall died. But the old man left his own legacy, touching hundreds of lives with his guide service, his sporting camp, and Camp Roosevelt. He'd helped build his hometown from a sleepy backwoods settlement to a bustling burgh. He inspired a president, and then spread Roosevelt's message of steadfast determination far and wide. He did his duty and worked a shift that few could match. Taking account of his accomplishments and the life he lived, he was pleased for the most part. He had few regrets, and even changed his mind about Elkhorn.

"We were all a very happy family at Elkhorn Ranch those two years we spent there with Theodore Roosevelt," he wrote.[29] "We were glad to get back home—gladder, I guess, than about anything that had ever happened to us," he explained in his memoirs. "And yet we were melancholy for with all the hardships and work it was a very happy life we had all lived together. I guess we have all thought all our lives since that it was the happiest time that any of us had ever known."[30]

Roosevelt had expressed similar thoughts. At the end of a letter documenting the travails of his western venture he had tacked on a note suggesting he'd do it all over again: "We had pretty good fun at the old ranch at any rate."[31]

Happy as he was, Sewall harbored a desire for an even simpler time even closer to nature. Much like his friend Theodore Roosevelt.

"I have always been glad that I was destined to live at this time," he wrote in his memoir. "Although I feel that I should have enjoyed living a hundred years sooner. All the tales of the pioneers are dear to me, and I've always believed I could have gotten along peaceably with the Indians of old.

"The old people are nearly all gone, and as I look about me at the few like myself who are left, I am reminded of the old-time forests: They too are gone, except for some great pine or spruce that still towers, alone, undaunted by wind and weather—gnarled old landmarks seeming to proclaim to the world that they have fulfilled their mission."[32]

William Wingate Sewall (1845–1930)

Donna Davidge-Bonham / Sewall House

Epilogue

Bill Sewall's death was not only painful but utterly exhausting for his widow. Mary had spent so much time doting on her husband, fretting about him and generally living in an anxious state, that she was all but spent when he finally passed away. She returned to Island Falls with Bill's casket the same night he died and said later that she hardly remembered making the trip.[1] Some of her children accompanied her on the train, others met her at stations along the route. Just as she had taken care of Bill, they now looked after her.

Harriet wanted her mother to return to New Hampshire with her after the funeral, but Mary was convinced she was needed in Island Falls; someone had to make sure that Bill's affairs were in order. She'd stay, with her sons Fred and Merrill to check on her, and she'd take in boarders once again at the Sewall House.

About a year later, Harriet received a letter from her brothers saying that Mary was seriously ill with pneumonia. Her daughters rushed north to be with her, and they all decided the best course would be for Mary to move in with her daughter Nancy, in Biddeford, Maine. Kittie lived close by. The doctors there were concerned not only about the lung infection, but also her heart. Mary was diagnosed with a condition known as endocarditis, a heart inflammation that the doctors suspected she'd probably had all her life.

Mrs. Sewall recuperated through the spring and was afterward persuaded to move yet again. This time she went to live with Harriet, who had a large new home in New Hampshire.

In the summer of 1932, Harriet took her mother back to Island Falls for a two-week stay. As they approached the hamlet on the Mattawamkeag, seeing first Silver Ridge then Golden Ridge, and then the village of Island Falls itself, Mary was delighted and relieved to be surrounded once again by the Aroostook countryside. She was even more thrilled to sleep in the home where she had spent so many happy years. It was warm and comfortable, and she felt a familiar presence: "William was there, too, not really but very pleasantly in her mind, as though he'd soon come in from the sheds or the post office."[2] She didn't want to leave ever again. But leave she did, when Harriet and her family had to return to the Granite State.

Once again, Mary tried to lose herself in the lives of her daughter and grand-children, but her heart remained back in Island Falls. That fall and winter it seemed to Harriet that her mother was fading, becoming ever more fragile, concerns she shared in letters to her siblings after the holidays. By February, Mary was bedridden for much of the time. Her ailing heart finally gave out on May 7, 1933.

Bill and Mary Sewall had witnessed the finest years of their beloved Island Falls. About the time Mary died, the economic life of the town began to slow down appreciably. The largest employer, the F.W. Hunt tannery, purchased from Proctor and Hunt, closed its doors in 1926. This was a difficult blow for Island Falls, which had already lost several of its other mills.

The town the Sewalls built had reached its zenith in about 1916, when local lumberman and entrepreneur Carl Milliken was elected governor of Maine and more than 1,680 people called the place home. After the tannery closed, Island Falls began to shed residents quickly—two hundred moved out—and its popu-lation has been on the decline ever since. Today only about eight hundred live there, though it remains a remote and pleasant place, that more and more visitors from away seem to be finding for wild recreation. Sewall and Roosevelt would feel comfortable walking down the street today, and they'd find a trove of memora-bilia about themselves at the Island Falls Historical Society's Museum on Burleigh Street. Tucked away in an old jail building, the place has pictures, clippings, and collectibles related to Sewall.

With the advent of the automobile, train service also began to diminish. The Bangor and Aroostook made its last stop in Island Falls in 1961, and the train station that Bill Sewall had been so excited to see built was torn down in 1970. Several downtown businesses burned over the years, including the hotels. Others simply closed. Camp Roosevelt moved to Pleasant Lake and ceased serving meals during the Second World War, when it was pressed into service as a military camp. The other sporting camps that had grown up in the wake of Hook Point Camps also saw their fortunes decline. Most went under, although people from away can still find remote Mattawamkeag recreation at such places as Birch Point Resort and Bear Creek Lodge.

Merrill Sewall continued to run his family's camps, while his brother, Fred, worked in the woods, just as their father had. Bill once had said that he hoped seeing Washington and attending the inauguration of President Roosevelt would inspire his children, "especially Fred," toward some "fine ambition,"[3] but the oldest Sewall boy had too much of the old guide in him and was tugged inexorably into the woods. Merrill died in 1961; Fred made it almost to the century mark, dying at the age of ninety-two in 1978. His son, George, continued to run the family camps until he was no longer able to make a go of them, selling the property to an out-of-state family.

Each of the three girls—Kittie, Nancy, and Harriet—married and moved to southern Maine and New Hampshire, returning to Island Falls for visits in the summer. Nancy eventually moved back to the Sewall House, living there until 1996, and keeping the family history alive. She was 101 when she died. All of the Sewall children had children of their own—at the time Bill died he was grandfather to ten.

The Sewall House remains in the family and to this day continues the tradition of hospitality begun by Levi Sewall in the 1840s. Donna Davidge, the fifth generation in the house, runs the lovely old place as a yoga retreat, splitting her time between Island Falls and New York City.

As for the Roosevelts, they continued to pay visits to Island Falls for years—a member of the family even owned an island in Mattawamkeag Lake as late as the 1960s. And the lives of the two families remained entwined. TR's Cousin Emlen returned at least once, and Harriet Sewall was so taken with him she named one of her sons after him.

And the story of the Sewalls and Roosevelts took an interesting turn in the 1960s. In an upstairs room at the Sewall House, Donna Davidge found an undated newspaper clipping that offers an intriguing bit of social news: Sometime in the early sixties, in New York City, a Mr. Tingey Sewall, son of James Wingate Sewall, of Bangor, Maine, married Lucy Margaret Roosevelt, daughter of W. Emlen Roosevelt, of New York. Neither of the newlyweds was directly descended from or even closely related to William Wingate Sewall or Theodore Roosevelt, but still, one can imagine that the two lifelong friends would have applauded the linking of their family names.

Chapter Notes

Introduction (pages 9–11)

1. Hermann Hagedorn, *The Boy's Life of Theodore Roosevelt* (N.Y. and London: Harper and Brothers, 1918), 1.
2. William Wingate Sewall, *Bill Sewall's Story of T.R.* (N.Y. and London: Harper and Brothers, 1919), 4–5.
3. Sewall, *Bill Sewall's Story*, 2.
4. Hagedorn, *The Boy's Life*, 58.
5. Hagedorn, *The Boy's Life*, 55–56.
6. Corinne Roosevelt Robinson, *My Brother, Theodore Roosevelt* (N.Y.: Charles Scribner's Sons, 1921), 111.
7. Robinson, *My Brother*, 92.
8. Daniel Henderson, *Great-Heart: The Life Story of Theodore Roosevelt* (N.Y. : Alfred A. Knopf, 1919), 7.
9. Carleton Putnam, *Theodore Roosevelt, Volume 1, The Formative Years*, (N.Y.: Charles Scribner's Sons, 1958), 123.
10. Putnam, *Theodore Roosevelt*, 158.
11. H.W. Brands, TR: *The Last Romantic* (N.Y.: Basic Books, 1998), 89.
12. Ibid.
13. *Autograph Magazine* (October 2003), 29.
14. Theodore Roosevelt, "My Debt to Maine," in *Maine: My State* (Lewiston, Me.: Maine Writers Research Club, 1919), 17.
15. William Henry Harbaugh, *The Life and Times of Theodore Roosevelt*, (N.Y.: Collier Books, 1966), 23.
16. Sewall, *Bill Sewall's Story*, introduction.

A Man to Know (pages 13–21)

1. Alvin Harlow, *Theodore Roosevelt, Strenuous American* (N.Y.: Julian Messner Publishers, 1943), 48.
2. U.S. Census, Island Falls, Aroostook County, Maine, 1880.
3. Ibid
4. Nina G. Sawyer, *Island Falls, Maine: 1872–1972* (Island Falls, Me.: Island Falls Historical Soc., 1972), 9.
5. William Wingate Sewall, *Bill Sewall's Story of T.R.* (N.Y. and London: Harper and Brothers, 1919), 2.
6. Sewall, *Bill Sewall's Story*, 2.
7. William Roscoe Thayer, *Theodore Roosevelt: An Intimate Biography* (Boston and N.Y.: Houghton Mifflin, 1919), 17.
8. Robert. M. Lindsell, *The Rail Lines of Northern New England* (Pepperell, Mass.: Branch Line Press, 2000), 217.
9. Carleton Putnam, *Theodore Roosevelt: Volume 1, The Formative Years* (N.Y., Charles Scribner's Sons, 1958), 153.
10. Theodore Roosevelt, 1878 Private Diary, Theodore Roosevelt Collection, Houghton Library, Harvard Univ., Cambridge, Mass., 23.

11. Harriett [Harriet] H. Miller, *Mary Alice Sherman Sewall: A Biography Chinked with Fiction* (Island Falls, Me.: privately published, 1984), 31.
12. U.S. Census, Island Falls, 1880.
13. Theodore Roosevelt, "My Debt to Maine," in *Maine: My State* (Lewiston, Me.: Maine Writers Research Club, 1919), 19.
14. Roosevelt, "My Debt to Maine," 19.
15. Edward Wiggin and George H. Collins, *History of Aroostook* (Presque Isle, Me.: Star Herald Press, 1922), 211.
16. Sewall, *Bill Sewall's Story*, 1–2.
17. Sewall, *Bill Sewall's Story*, 2.
18. Edmund Morris, *The Rise of Theodore Roosevelt* (N.Y.: Modern Library, Random House, 1979) 75.
19. Sewall, *Bill Sewall's Story*, 2.
20. Putnam, *Theodore Roosevelt: Volume 1*, 154.
21. Sewall, *Bill Sewall's Story*, 2–3.
22. William Henry Harbaugh, *The Life and Times of Theodore Roosevelt* (N.Y.: Collier Books, 1966), 214.
23. Sawyer, *Island Falls, Maine*, 26.
24. Roosevelt, 1878 Private Diary, 23.
25. Sewall, *Bill Sewall's Story*, 5.
26. Roosevelt, 1878 Private Diary, 23.
27. Ibid.
28. Roosevelt, 1878 Private Diary, 24.
29. "Roosevelt and the Rooster," *Atlanta Constitution* (October 9, 1901), 6.
30. Sewall, *Bill Sewall's Story*, 5.
31. Daniel Henderson, *Great-Heart: The Life Story of Theodore Roosevelt* (N.Y.: Alfred A. Knopf, 1919), 6.
32. Sewall, *Bill Sewall's Story*, 3.
33. Putnam, *Theodore Roosevelt: Volume 1*, 154–57.
34. Sewall, *Bill Sewall's Story*, 5.
35. Roosevelt, 1878 Private Diary, 24.
36. Roosevelt, 1878 Private Diary, 25.
37. Roosevelt, "My Debt to Maine," 19.
38. Roosevelt, 1878 Private Diary, 25.
39. Ibid.
40. Ibid.
41. Sewall, *Bill Sewall's Story*, 5.

The Nature of New York (pages 23–29)

1. Theodore Roosevelt, *Theodore Roosevelt: An Autobiography* (N.Y.: Macmillan, 1913), 33.
2. Roosevelt, *Autobiography*, 33.
3. Ibid.
4. Roosevelt, *Autobiography*, 1.
5. Daniel Henderson, *Great-Heart: The Life Story of Theodore Roosevelt* (N.Y.: Alfred A. Knopf, 1919), 4.
6. Roosevelt, *Autobiography*, 7.
7. Theodore Roosevelt, *Letters from Theodore Roosevelt to Anna Roosevelt Cowles, 1870–1918* (N.Y.: Charles Scribner's Sons, 1924), 11.
8. Henderson, *Great-Heart*, 5.

9. Roosevelt, *Autobiography*, 17.

10. Hermann Hagedorn, *The Boy's Life of Theodore Roosevelt* (N.Y. and London: Harper and Brothers, 1918), 28.

11. Elting E. Morrison, ed., *Letters of Theodore Roosevelt, Volume 1, The Years of Preparation, 1868–1898* (Cambridge, Mass.: Harvard Univ. Press, 1951), 17.

12. David McCullough, *Mornings on Horseback: The Story of an Extraordinary Family, a Vanished Way of Life, and the Unique Child Who Became Theodore Roosevelt* (N.Y.: Simon and Schuster, 1982), 31.

13. Roosevelt, *Autobiography*, 13.

14. Roosevelt, *Autobiography*, 8.

15. Ibid.

16. Roosevelt, *Autobiography*, 12.

17. Roosevelt, *Autobiography*, 14.

18. Corinne Roosevelt Robinson, *My Brother, Theodore Roosevelt* (N.Y.: Charles Scribner's Sons, 1921), 17.

19. Roosevelt, *Autobiography*, 20.

20. Roosevelt, *Autobiography*, 12–13.

21. Roosevelt, *Autobiography*, 20, 30.

22. Roosevelt, *Autobiography*, 32.

Pine Tree Pioneers (pages 31–45)

1. William Wingate Sewall. *Recollections of William Wingate Sewall of Island Falls Maine: 1845–1930* (Island Falls, Me.: privately published, copyright Harriett [Harriet] S. Harmon and Harriett [Harriet] H. Miller, 1972), 21.

2. Henry Sweetser Burrage, *Maine in the Northeastern Boundary Controversy* (Portland, Me.: State of Maine, 1919), 29.

3. Richard W. Judd, *Aroostook: A Century of Logging* (Orono: Univ. of Maine Press, 1989), 2.

4. Judd, *Aroostook*, 2.

5. Sewall genealogy from http://www.genealogy.bsewall.com.

6. http://www.aroostook.me.com.

7. *Report of an Exploration and Survey of the Territory on the Aroostook River, during the Spring and Autumn of 1838* (Augusta, Me.: Smith and Robinson, 1839), 77–78.

8. Sewall, *Recollections*, 1–10.

9. Nina G. Sawyer, *Island Falls, Maine: 1872–1972* (Island Falls, Me.: Island Falls Historical Soc., 1972), 6.

10. Edward Wiggin and George H. Collins, *History of Aroostook* (Presque Isle, Me.: Star Herald Press, 1922), 207.

11. Sewall, *Recollections*, 10.

12. William S. Dutton, "The Big Woods Are Friendly If You Know 'Em Well Enough," *The American Magazine* (1926), 54.

13. Sewall, *Recollections*, 29.

14. Ibid.

15. Dutton, "The Big Woods," 55.

16. Sewall, *Recollections*, 29.

17. Sewall, *Recollections*, 47.

18. Sewall, *Recollections*, 46.

19. Sewall, *Recollections*, 33.

20. Lew Dietz, *The Allagash* (N.Y.: Holt, Rinehart, and Winston, 1968), 226.

21. Sewall, *Recollections*, 49.

22. Sewall, *Recollections*, 50–52.

23. Sewall, *Recollections*, 61.

24. Sewall, *Recollections*, 67.

25. Lawrence C. Allin and Richard W. Judd, "Creating Maine's Resource Economy: 1783–1861," in *Maine: The Pine Tree State from Prehistory to the Present* (Orono: Univ. of Maine Press, 1995), 267.

26. Judd, *Aroostook*, 70–71.

27. Sawyer, *Island Falls, Maine*, 22–27.

28. Sewall, *Recollections*, 66.

A Grander, More Beautiful Sight (pages 47–52)

1. Theodore Roosevelt, 1879 Private Diary,, Theodore Roosevelt Collection, Houghton Library, Harvard Univ., Cambridge, Mass., 3.

2. Roosevelt, 1879 Private Diary, 3.

3. Theodore Roosevelt, *Letters from Theodore Roosevelt to Anna Roosevelt Cowles, 1870–1918* (N.Y.: Charles Scribner's Sons, 1924), 32.

4. Roosevelt, 1879 Private Diary, 4.

5. Ibid.

6. Ibid.

7. Roosevelt, *Letters*, 32.

8. Roosevelt, 1879 Private Diary, 4.

9. Ibid.

10. Roosevelt, 1879 Private Diary, 5.

11. Ibid.

12. Ibid.

13. William Wingate Sewall, *Bill Sewall's Story of T.R.* (N.Y. and London: Harper and Brothers, 1919), 5–6.

14. Sewall, *Bill Sewall's Story*, 6.

15. Roosevelt, 1879 Private Diary, 6.

16. Ibid.

17. "Old Bill Sewall," *Hartford Courant* (September 6, 1902), 14.

18. Sewall, *Bill Sewall's Story*, 6.

19. Roosevelt, *Letters*, 32.

20. Ibid.

21. Ibid.

22. Roosevelt, 1879 Private Diary, 6.

23. Theodore Roosevelt, "My Debt to Maine," in *Maine: My State* (Lewiston, Me.: Maine Writers Research Club, 1919), 19.

24. Roosevelt, 1879 Private Diary, 6.

25. Ibid.

26. Letter from Theodore Roosevelt to Martha Bulloch Roosevelt, March 10, 1879, Theodore Roosevelt Collection, Houghton Library, Harvard Univ., Cambridge, Mass.

Tough as a Pine Knot (pages 53–61)

1. Theodore Roosevelt, 1879 Private Diary, Theodore Roosevelt Collection, Houghton Library, Harvard Univ., Cambridge, Mass., 21

2. Roosevelt, 1879 Private Diary, 21.

3. "Origins of Weasel Words," *New York Times* (September 2, 1916), 4.

4. Theodore Roosevelt, "My Debt to Maine," in *Maine: My State* (Lewiston, Me.: Maine Writers Research Club, 1919), 20.

5. William Wingate Sewall. *Recollections of William Wingate Sewall of Island Falls Maine: 1845–1930* (Island Falls, Me.: privately published, copyright Harriett [Harriet] S. Harmon and Harriett [Harriet] H. Miller, 1972), 81.

6. Sewall, *Recollections*, 81.

7. Roosevelt, 1879 Private Diary, 21.

8. John Neff, *Katahdin: An Historic Journey: Legends, Exploration, and Preservation of Maine's Highest Peak* (Boston: Appalachian Mountain Club Books, 2006), 85.

9. Roosevelt, 1879 Private Diary, 22.

10. Ibid.

11. William Wingate Sewall, *Bill Sewall's Story of T.R.* (N.Y. and London: Harper and Brothers, 1919), 7.

12. Roosevelt, 1879 Private Diary, 22.

13. Ibid.

14. Ibid.

15. Theodore Roosevelt, *Letters from Theodore Roosevelt to Anna Roosevelt Cowles, 1870–1918* (N.Y.: Charles Scribner's Sons, 1924), 7–8.

16. Roosevelt, *Letters*, 7–8.

17. Daniel Henderson, *Great-Heart: The Life Story of Theodore Roosevelt* (N.Y.: Alfred A. Knopf, 1919), 6.

18. Roosevelt, 1879 Private Diary, 22.

19. Ibid.

20. Ibid.

21. Roosevelt, 1879 Private Diary, 23.

22. Roosevelt, *Letters*, 7–8.

23. Roosevelt, 1879 Private Diary, 23.

24. Ibid.

25. Ibid.

26. Ibid.

27. Roosevelt, 1879 Private Diary, 24.

28. Ibid.

29. Ibid.

30. Roosevelt, *Letters*, 33–34.

31. Roosevelt, 1879 Private Diary, 24.

32. Ibid.

33. Ibid.

34. "Roosevelt Yarns," *Los Angeles Times* (January 8, 1899), A5.

35. Roosevelt, 1879 Private Diary, 24.

36. Roosevelt, 1879 Private Diary, 25.

37. Ibid.

38. "Roosevelt Yarns," A5.

39. Roosevelt, *Letters*, 33.

40. Roosevelt, 1879 Private Diary, 25.

41. Ibid.

42. Ibid.

43. Roosevelt, 1879 Private Diary, 26.

44. Ibid.

Harvard Cool (pages 63–69)

1. Theodore Roosevelt, 1879 Private Diary, Theodore Roosevelt Collection, Houghton Library, Harvard Univ., Cambridge. Mass., 22.

2. H.W. Brands, *T.R.: The Last Romantic* (N.Y.: Basic Books, 1997), 59.

3. Lew Dietz, *The Allagash* (N.Y.: Holt, Rinehart and Winston, 1968), 177.

4. Theodore Roosevelt, *Theodore Roosevelt: An Autobiography* (N.Y.: Macmillan, 1913), 4.

5. Theodore Roosevelt, "My Debt to Maine," in *Maine: My State* (Lewiston, Me.: Maine Writers Research Club, 1919), 17.

6. William Wingate Sewall, *Bill Sewall's Story of T.R.* (N.Y. and London: Harper and Brothers Publishers, 1919), 8.

7. Theodore Roosevelt, *Letters from Theodore Roosevelt to Anna Roosevelt Cowles, 1870–1918* (N.Y.: Charles Scribner's Sons, 1924), 12.

8. Kathleen Dalton, *Theodore Roosevelt: A Strenuous Life* (N.Y.: Vintage Books, 2004), 56.

9. Roosevelt, *Letters*, 16.

10. Roosevelt, *Autobiography*, 26.

11. Roosevelt, *Letters*, 13.

12. Roosevelt, *Letters*, 16.

13. Carleton Putnam, *Theodore Roosevelt: Volume 1, The Formative Years* (N.Y.: Charles Scribner's Sons, 1958), 126.

14. Putnam, *Theodore Roosevelt*, 143.

15. John W. Tyler, *The Life of William McKinley: Soldier, Statesman and President* (Philadelphia: P. W. Siegler and Co., 1901), 496.

16. Roosevelt, *Letters*, 20.

17. Alvin F. Harlow, *Theodore Roosevelt: Strenuous American* (N.Y.: Julian Messner Publishers, 1959), 41.

18. "Harvard Univ.," *Scribner's Magazine* (July 1876), 337–360.

19. Phillip Boffey, "Theodore Roosevelt at Harvard," *Harvard Crimson* (December 12, 1957).

20. Carleton Putnam Notes, Theodore Roosevelt Collection, Houghton Library, Harvard Univ., Cambridge, Mass., R110, P971.

21. Ibid.

22. Elting E. Morrison, ed., *Letters of Theodore Roosevelt, Vol. 1, The Years of Preparation, 1868–1898* (Cambridge, Mass.: Harvard Univ. Press, 1951), 24.

23. *Boston Saturday Evening Gazette* (November 9, 1879), 2–3.

24. Roosevelt, *Autobiography*, 31.

25. Perriton Maxwell, "An Anecdotal Portrait of Colonel Roosevelt," in *True Stories of Heroic Lives* (N.Y.: Funk and Wagnalls, 1899), 69–70.

26. Roosevelt, *Autobiography*, 31.

27. Roosevelt, *Autobiography*, 28–29.

28. Roosevelt, *Autobiography*, 29.

29. Roosevelt, *Autobiography*, 30.

30. Roosevelt, *Letters*, 25.

31. Ibid.

32. David McCullough, *Mornings on Horseback: The Story of an Extraordinary Family, a Vanished Way of Life, and the Unique Child Who Became Theodore Roosevelt* (N.Y.: Simon and Schuster, 1982), 190.

33. McCullough, *Mornings on Horseback*, 187.

34. Morrison, *Letters*, 31.

35. Putnam, *Theodore Roosevelt*, 148.

36. Putnam, *Theodore Roosevelt*, 151.

37. Putnam, *Theodore Roosevelt*, 149.

Playing the Frontier (pages 71–77)

1. David McCullough, *Mornings on Horseback: The Story of an Extraordinary Family, a Vanished Way of Life, and the Unique Child Who Became Theodore Roosevelt* (N.Y.: Simon and Schuster, 1982), 221.
2. Carleton Putnam, *Theodore Roosevelt: Volume 1, The Formative Years* (N.Y.: Charles Scribner's Sons, 1958), 168.
3. Elting E. Morrison, ed., *Letters of Theodore Roosevelt, Vol. 1, The Years of Preparation, 1868–1898* (Cambridge, Mass.: Harvard Univ. Press, 1951), 25–35.
4. Alvin F. Harlow, *Theodore Roosevelt: Strenuous American* (N.Y.: Julian Messner Publishers, 1959), 47.
5. Putnam, *Theodore Roosevelt*, 190.
6. Putnam, *Theodore Roosevelt*, 171.
7. Putnam, *Theodore Roosevelt*, 171–172.
8. Putnam, *Theodore Roosevelt*, 190.
9. Putnam, *Theodore Roosevelt*, 168.
10. Harlow, *Theodore Roosevelt*, 47.
11. Nathan Miller, *Theodore Roosevelt: A Life* (N.Y.: Harper Collins, 1994), 99.
12. Putnam, *Theodore Roosevelt*, 200.
13. Putnam, *Theodore Roosevelt*, 198.
14. "Bill Sewall Visits Roosevelt's Grave," *New York Times* (March 24, 1919), 8.
15. Putnam, *Theodore Roosevelt*, 200–201.
16. Putnam, *Theodore Roosevelt*, 205.
17. Putnam, *Theodore Roosevelt*, 208.
18. Theodore Roosevelt, *Letters from Theodore Roosevelt to Anna Roosevelt Cowles, 1870–1918* (N.Y.: Charles Scribner's Sons, 1924), 38–39.
19. Putnam, *Theodore Roosevelt*, 207.
20. *Brookline (Mass.) Chronicle* (October 30, 1880), 31.
21. Hermann Hagedorn, *Roosevelt and Gorringe, Roosevelt in the Badlands* (N.Y.: Houghton Mifflin, 1921), 8–9.
22. Joseph Nimms, Jr., Range and Ranch Cattle Business of the United States. Part III of the Report on the Internal Commerce of the United States (U.S. Treasury Department, May 6, 1885), 98.
23. Nimms, Range and Ranch Cattle Business, appendix.
24. Theodore Roosevelt, Letter dated September 8, 1883, Roosevelt Collection, Houghton Library, Harvard Univ., Cambridge, Mass.
25. Ibid.
26. Theodore Roosevelt, *Theodore Roosevelt: An Autobiography* (N.Y.: Macmillan, 1913), 106.
27. Jim Posewitz, "How the King's Deer Became the People's Deer," *Delta Waterfowl Magazine* (Summer 2008).
28. Paul Grondahl, *I Rose Like A Rocket: The Political Education of Theodore Roosevelt* (N.Y.: Simon and Schuster, 2004), 120.
29. Roosevelt, *Letters*, 59.
30. Hagedorn interviews, Theodore Roosevelt Collection, Houghton Library, Harvard Univ., Cambridge, Mass., 720.
31. Hagedorn interviews, 714.
32. Chester L. Brooks and Ray A. Mattison, *Theodore Roosevelt and the Dakota Badlands* (Washington, D.C.: National Park Service, 1958), not paginated.
33. Hermann Hagedorn, *The Boy's Life of Theodore Roosevelt* (N.Y.: Harper and Brothers Publishers, 1918), 103.

Light Comes In, Light Goes Out (pages 79–87)

1. "Roosevelt Yarns" *Los Angeles Times* (January 8, 1899), A5.
2. Ibid.
3. Harriet H. Miller, *Mary Alice Sherman Sewall: A Biography Chinked with Fiction* (Island Falls, Me.: privately published, 1984), 26.
4. Miller, *Mary Alice Sherman Sewall*, 26.
5. Ibid.
6. Ibid.
7. Miller, *Mary Alice Sherman Sewall*, 27.
8. Miller, *Mary Alice Sherman Sewall*, 26.
9. Miller, *Mary Alice Sherman Sewall*, 29.
10. Miller, *Mary Alice Sherman Sewall*, 28.
11. Ibid.
12. Miller, *Mary Alice Sherman Sewall*, 30–31.
13. William Wingate Sewall, *Recollections of William Wingate Sewall of Island Falls Maine: 1845–1930* (Island Falls, Me.: privately published, 1972), 76–80.
14. Miller, *Mary Alice Sherman Sewall*, 31.
15. Ibid.
16. Miller, *Mary Alice Sherman Sewall*, 32.
17. Miller, *Mary Alice Sherman Sewall*, 31.
18. Elting E. Morrison, ed., *Letters of Theodore Roosevelt, Vol. 1, The Years of Preparation, 1868–1898* (Cambridge, Mass.: Harvard Univ. Press, 1951), 66–67.
19. William Wingate Sewall, *Bill Sewall's Story of T.R.* (N.Y. and London: Harper and Brothers, 1919), 11–12.
20. Theodore Roosevelt, 1884 Diary, Theodore Roosevelt Collection, Houghton Library, Harvard Univ., Cambridge, Mass. 1.
21. Miller, *Mary Alice Sherman Sewall*, 32.
22. Sewall, *Bill Sewall's Story*, 11.
23. Theodore Roosevelt, Letter dated March 26, 1884, Theodore Roosevelt Collection, Howard Gotlieb Archival Research Center, Boston Univ.
24. Sewall, *Bill Sewall's Story*, 12–13.
25. Miller, *Mary Alice Sherman Sewall*, 33.
26. Sewall, *Bill Sewall's Story*, 13–14.
27. Miller, *Mary Alice Sherman Sewall*, 34.
28. Miller, *Mary Alice Sherman Sewall*, 35.
29. Ibid.
30. Ibid.
31. Ibid.

Badlands Babies (pages 89–97)

1. William Wingate Sewall, *Bill Sewall's Story of T.R.* (N.Y. and London: Harper and Brothers, 1919), 14.
2. Sewall, *Bill Sewall's Story*, 17.
3. Sewall, *Bill Sewall's Story*, 15.
4. Sewall, *Bill Sewall's Story*, 16.
5. Joseph Nimms, Jr., Range and Ranch Cattle Business of the United States, Part III of the Report on the Internal Commerce of the United States (U.S. Treasury Department, May 6, 1885), 8.

6. Medora history from http://www.medora.com, Web site of the Theodore Roosevelt Medora Foundation, Medora, N.D.

7. W. T. Dantz, Hagedorn interviews, Theodore Roosevelt Collection, Houghton Library, Harvard Univ., Cambridge. Mass.

8. Theodore Roosevelt, *Letters from Theodore Roosevelt to Anna Roosevelt Cowles, 1870–1918* (N.Y.: Charles Scribner's Sons, 1924), 60.

9. William W. Sewall and Mary Sewall, *Life at Roosevelt's Elkhorn Ranch: The Letters of William W. and Mary Sewall*, ed. Ray H. Mattison (Bismarck (N.D.) Tribune, 1960), 5. Reprinted from *North Dakota Historical Soc. Quarterly* 27, nos. 3 and 4.

10. Hermann Hagedorn, *Roosevelt and Gorringe, Roosevelt in the Badlands* (N.Y.: Houghton Mifflin, 1921), 163.

11. Sewall, *Life at Elkhorn*, 9.

12. Hagedorn, *Roosevelt and Gorringe*, 163.

13. Sewall, *Bill Sewall's Story*, 16–19.

14. Sewall, *Life at Elkhorn*, 5.

15. William Wingate Sewall, *Recollections of William Wingate Sewall of Island Falls Maine: 1845–1930* (Island Falls, Me.: privately published, 1972), 86.

16. Usher Lloyd Burdick, "The Life and Exploits of John Goodall," *McKenzie County (N.D.) Farmer* (1931), 11.

17. Sewall, *Bill Sewall's Story*, 18.

18. Sewall, *Life at Elkhorn*, 5.

19. Sewall, *Bill Sewall's Story*, 19–20.

20. Hermann Hagedorn, *The Boy's Life of Theodore Roosevelt* (N.Y. and London: Harper and Brothers, 1918), 107.

21. "The Passing of a Grand Old Man," *Bangor Daily News* (March 17, 1930).

22. Hagedorn, *Roosevelt and Gorringe*, 166. In his accounts of such conversations, Hagedorn liked to make Sewall appear the backwoodsman.

23. Sewall, *Life at Elkhorn*, 27.

24. Sewall, *Bill Sewall's Story*, 22–24.

25. Sewall, *Bill Sewall's Story*, 21.

26. Sewall, *Bill Sewall's Story*, 45–46.

27. Sewall, *Bill Sewall's Story*, 22.

28. Sewall, *Bill Sewall's Story*, 19.

29. Sewall, *Life at Elkhorn*, 9.

30. Sewall, *Bill Sewall's Story*, 25.

31. Harriet H. Miller, *Mary Alice Sherman Sewall: A Biography Chinked with Fiction* (Island Falls, Me.: privately published, 1984), 36.

32. Sewall, *Life at Elkhorn*, 6.

33. Sewall, *Life at Elkhorn*, 14.

34. Sewall, *Life at Elkhorn*, 7.

35. Sewall, *Life at Elkhorn*, 5.

36. Sewall, *Life at Elkhorn*, 6.

37. Sewall, *Life at Elkhorn*, 38.

38. Sewall, *Life at Elkhorn*, 14.

39. Sewall, *Bill Sewall's Story*, 47.

40. Henry F. Pringle, *Theodore Roosevelt: A Biography* (Whitefish, Mont.: Kessinger Publishing, 2005) 93.

41. Corinne Roosevelt Robinson, *My Brother, Theodore Roosevelt* (N.Y.: Charles Scribner's Sons, 1921), 127.

Cowpunching (pages 99–108)

1. William W. Sewall and Mary Sewall, *Life at Roosevelt's Elkhorn Ranch: The Letters of William W. and Mary Sewall*, ed. Ray H. Mattison (*Bismarck (N.D.) Tribune*, 1960), 12. Reprinted from *North Dakota Historical Soc. Quarterly* 27, nos. 3 and 4.
2. Sewall, *Life at Elkhorn*, 12.
3. Sewall, *Life at Elkhorn*, 17.
4. William Wingate Sewall, *Bill Sewall's Story of T.R.* (N.Y. and London: Harper and Brothers, 1919), 37.
5. Sewall, *Life at Elkhorn*, 17.
6. Hermann Hagedorn, *Roosevelt and Gorringe, Roosevelt in the Badlands* (N.Y.: Houghton Mifflin, 1921), 481.
7. Harriet H. Miller, *Mary Alice Sherman Sewall: A Biography Chinked with Fiction* (Island Falls, Me.: privately published, 1984), 37.
8. Sewall, *Life at Elkhorn*, 18.
9. Miller, *Mary Alice Sherman Sewall*, 37.
10. Miller, *Mary Alice Sherman Sewall*, 38.
11. Sewall, *Bill Sewall's Story*, 38.
12. Sewall, *Bill Sewall's Story*, 39.
13. Miller, *Mary Alice Sherman Sewall*, 38.
14. Elting E. Morrison, ed., *Letters of Theodore Roosevelt, Vol. 1, The Years of Preparation, 1868–1898* (Cambridge, Mass.: Harvard Univ. Press, 1951), 100.
15. Theodore Roosevelt, "My Debt to Maine," in *Maine: My State* (Lewiston, Me.: Maine Writers Research Club, 1919), 21.
16. Miller, *Mary Alice Sherman Sewall*, 41.
17. Sewall, *Life at Elkhorn*, 25.
18. Sewall, *Life at Elkhorn*, 34.
19. Sewall, *Life at Elkhorn*, 26.
20. Theodore Roosevelt, Letter dated December 2, 1885, Theodore Roosevelt Collection, Howard Gotlieb Archival Research Center, Boston Univ.
21. Hermann Hagedorn, *The Boy's Life of Theodore Roosevelt* (N.Y. and London: Harper and Brothers, 1918), 115.
22. Hermann Hagedorn, *Roosevelt in the Badlands* (N.Y.: Houghton Mifflin, 1921), 258).
23. Hermann Hagedorn, Hagedorn notes, Theodore Roosevelt Collection, Houghton Library, Harvard Univ., Cambridge, Mass.
24. Sewall, *Bill Sewall's Story*, 27–29.
25. Sewall, *Life at Elkhorn*, 29.
26. Sewall, *Life at Elkhorn*, 29.
27. Miller, *Mary Alice Sherman Sewall*, 41.
28. Sewall, *Bill Sewall's Story*, 66.
29. Sewall, *Life at Elkhorn*, 30.
30. Hagedorn, Hagedorn notes, 3.
31. Hagedorn, *Roosevelt and Gorringe*, 369.
32. Sewall, *Life at Elkhorn*, 30.
33. "Roosevelt Yarns," *Los Angeles Times* (January 8, 1899), A5.
34. Sewall, *Life at Elkhorn*, 31.
35. Ibid.
36. Ibid.
37. Ibid.
38. Sewall, *Bill Sewall's Story*, 84.
39. Sewall, *Bill Sewall's Story*, 85.
40. Sewall, *Life at Elkhorn*, 33.

The Beef (pages 109–113)

1. William Wingate Sewall, *Bill Sewall's Story of T.R.* (N.Y. and London: Harper and Brothers, 1919), 39.
2. Sewall, *Bill Sewall's Story*, 91.
3. Harriet H. Miller, *Mary Alice Sherman Sewall: A Biography Chinked with Fiction* (Island Falls, Me.: privately published, 1984), 42.
4. Ibid.
5. Miller, *Mary Alice Sherman Sewall*, 36.
6. William W. Sewall and Mary Sewall, *Life at Roosevelt's Elkhorn Ranch: The Letters of William W. and Mary Sewall*, ed. Ray H. Mattison (*Bismarck (N.D.) Tribune*, 1960), 27. Reprinted from *North Dakota Historical Soc. Quarterly* 27, nos. 3 and 4.
7. Sewall, *Life at Elkhorn*, 26–27.
8. Sewall, *Life at Elkhorn*, 27.
9. Sewall, *Bill Sewall's Story*, 42.
10. Sewall, *Bill Sewall's Story*, 91.
11. Sewall, *Life at Elkhorn*, 37.
12. Miller, *Mary Alice Sherman Sewall*, 41.
13. Sewall, *Bill Sewall's Story*, 91–93.
14. Miller, *Mary Alice Sherman Sewall*, 42–43.
15. Sewall, *Bill Sewall's Story*, 93.
16. Corinne Roosevelt Robinson, *My Brother, Theodore Roosevelt* (N.Y.: Charles Scribner's Sons, 1921), 127.
17. Sewall, *Bill Sewall's Story*, 93.

Futures and Fame (pages 135–145)

1. Harriet H. Miller, *Mary Alice Sherman Sewall: A Biography Chinked with Fiction* (Island Falls, Me.: privately published, 1984), 43.
2. Miller, *Mary Alice Sherman Sewall*, 43.
3. Nina G. Sawyer, *Island Falls, Maine: 1872–1972* (Island Falls, Me.: Island Falls Historical Soc., 1972), 33.
4. Miller, *Mary Alice Sherman Sewall*, 44.
5. William Wingate Sewall, *Bill Sewall's Story of T.R.* (N.Y. and London: Harper and Brothers, 1919), 41.
6. William Roscoe Thayer, *Theodore Roosevelt: An Intimate Biography* (Boston and N.Y.: Houghton Mifflin, 1919), 57.
7. Alvin Harlow, *Theodore Roosevelt, Strenuous American* (N.Y.: Julian Messner Publishers, 1943), 24.
8. Elting E. Morrison, ed., *Letters of Theodore Roosevelt, Vol. 1, The Years of Preparation, 1868–1898* (Cambridge, Mass.: Harvard Univ. Press, 1951), 28.
9. *Time* (January 18, 1926).
10. "Soc. Topics of the Week," *New York Times* (November 7, 1886), 14.
11. "Roosevelt was Married in London," *Washington Post* (August 25, 1905), 6.
12. William Wingate Sewall, *Bill Sewall's Story of T.R.* (N.Y. and London: Harper and Brothers, 1919), 96–97.
13. North Dakota weather records at http://www.wday.com/weather/index.cfm.
14. North Dakota Tourism Division Web site, http://www.ndtourism.com/about/Culture-Heritage/legends/description-of-north-dakota-history/default.asp?ID=458.
15. Theodore Roosevelt, Letter dated July 10, 1887, Theodore Roosevelt Collection, Howard Gotlieb Archival Research Center, Boston Univ.
16. Theodore Roosevelt, *Letters from Theodore Roosevelt to Anna Roosevelt Cowles, 1870–1918* (N.Y.: Charles Scribner's Sons, 1924), 126–127.
17. Ibid.

18. Theodore Roosevelt, Letter dated October 13, 1889, Theodore Roosevelt Collection, Howard Gotlieb Archival Research Center, Boston Univ.

19. Howard Eaton, Letter dated March 22, 1888, Theodore Roosevelt Collection, Houghton Library, Harvard Univ., Cambridge, Mass.

20. Theodore Roosevelt, Letters dated October 20, 1890, and November 2, 1890, Theodore Roosevelt Collection, Howard Gotlieb Archival Research Center, Boston Univ.

21. Theodore Roosevelt, Letter dated December 26, 1887, Theodore Roosevelt Collection, Howard Gotlieb Archival Research Center, Boston Univ.

22. Theodore Roosevelt, Letter dated December 26, 1903, Theodore Roosevelt Collection, Howard Gotlieb Archival Research Center, Boston Univ.

23. Miller, *Mary Alice Sherman Sewall*, 77.

24. Sewall, *Bill Sewall's Story*, 101.

25. Theodore Roosevelt, Letter dated February 26, 1891, Theodore Roosevelt Collection, Howard Gotlieb Archival Research Center, Boston Univ.

26. Theodore Roosevelt, Letter dated April 17, 1891, Theodore Roosevelt Collection, Howard Gotlieb Archival Research Center, Boston Univ.

27. Theodore Roosevelt, Letter dated May 22, 1888, Theodore Roosevelt Collection, Howard Gotlieb Archival Research Center, Boston Univ.

28. Theodore Roosevelt, Letter dated October 13, 1889, Theodore Roosevelt Collection, Howard Gotlieb Archival Research Center, Boston Univ.

29. "Congressional Gossip," *Bryan (Ohio) Times* (March 19, 1903), 6.

30. Sewall, *Bill Sewall's Story*, 102.

31. Ibid.

32. "Roosevelt's Old Guide," *New York Times* (June 29, 1902), 1.

33. Theodore Roosevelt, Letter dated May 4, 1898, Theodore Roosevelt Collection, Howard Gotlieb Archival Research Center, Boston Univ.

34. Miller, *Mary Alice Sherman Sewall*, 52.

35. Harriett [Harriet] S. Harmon and Harriett [Harriet] H. Miller, *Recollections of William Wingate Sewall of Island Falls Maine: 1845–1930* (Island Falls, Me.: privately published, 1972), 84.

36. Sewall, *Bill Sewall's Story*, 100.

37. Ibid.

38. Theodore Roosevelt, Letter dated August 5, 1891, Theodore Roosevelt Collection, Howard Gotlieb Archival Research Center, Boston Univ.

39. Theodore Roosevelt, Letter dated February 11, 1892, Theodore Roosevelt Collection, Howard Gotlieb Archival Research Center, Boston Univ.

40. Miller, *Mary Alice Sherman Sewall*, 48–49.

41. Sewall, *Recollections*, 85.

42. Miller, *Mary Alice Sherman Sewall*, 54.

43. Ibid.

44. Miller, *Mary Alice Sherman Sewall*, 49.

45. Sewall, *Recollections*, 85.

46. Nina G. Sawyer, ed., *Island Falls, Maine: 1872–1972* (Island Falls, Me.: Island Falls Historical Soc., 1972), 33.

47. Ibid.

48. Miller, *Mary Alice Sherman Sewall*, 49.

49. Harmon and Miller, *Recollections*, 88.

50. Sewall, *Bill Sewall's Story*, 104.

51. Ibid.

52. Ibid.

53. "Roosevelt Yarns," *Los Angeles Times* (January 8, 1899), A5.

I Want to See Roosevelt (pages 147–155)

1. Harriet H. Miller, *Mary Alice Sherman Sewall: A Biography Chinked with Fiction* (Island Falls, Me.: privately published, 1984), 56.
2. Edmund Morris, *The Rise of Theodore Roosevelt* (N.Y.: Ballantine Books, 1980), 740.
3. Miller, *Mary Alice Sherman Sewall*, 56.
4. "Roosevelt's Old Guide," *New York Times* (June 29, 1902).
5. Theodore Roosevelt, Letter dated May 13, 1901, Theodore Roosevelt Collection, Howard Gotlieb Archival Research Center, Boston Univ.
6. William Wingate Sewall, *Bill Sewall's Story of T.R.* (N.Y. and London: Harper and Brothers, 1919), 107–108.
7. "Preaches National Morality," *New York Times* (August 28, 1902).
8. Miller, *Mary Alice Sherman Sewall*, 57.
9. "Old 'Bill' Sewall, the Most Enthusiastic Roosevelt Man in Maine," *Hartford (Conn.) Courant* (September 6, 1902), 14. Reprint of article originally published in the *New York Tribune*.
10. Sewall, *Bill Sewall's Story*, 109.
11. Unattributed clipping, Sewall House collection, Island Falls, Me.
12. Sewall, *Bill Sewall's Story*, 109.
13. Miller, *Mary Alice Sherman Sewall*, 58.
14. Sewall, *Bill Sewall's Story*, 110.
15. Theodore Roosevelt, Letter dated September 11, 1902, Theodore Roosevelt Collection, Howard Gotlieb Archival Research Center, Boston Univ.
16. Nina G. Sawyer, ed., *Island Falls, Maine: 1872–1972* (Island Falls, Me.: Island Falls Historical Soc., 1972), 109.
17. Sewall, *Bill Sewall's Story*, 110.
18. Miller, *Mary Alice Sherman Sewall*, 58.
19. Sewall, *Bill Sewall's Story*, 111.
20. Miller, *Mary Alice Sherman Sewall*, 58.
21. Miller, *Mary Alice Sherman Sewall*, 59.
22. "Bill Sewall," *Boston Globe* (February 7, 1903), 8.
23. "'Bill' Sewall at Capitol," *New York Times* (February 7, 1903), 3.
24. Miller, *Mary Alice Sherman Sewall*, 59.
25. Sewall, *Bill Sewall's Story*, 111.
26. "Roosevelt Boys to Hunt," *New York Times* (February 23, 1903).
27. "Bill Sewall of Maine," *Boston Globe* (February 7, 1903).
28. "Enjoyed Vacation," *Boston Globe* (February 13, 1903), 6.
29. Theodore Roosevelt, "My Debt to Maine," in *Maine: My State* (Lewiston, Me.: Maine Writers Research Club, 1919), 22.
30. Miller, *Mary Alice Sherman Sewall*, 58.
31. "The Sewalls in New York," *New York Herald* (February 25, 1903), 18.
32. Unattributed newspaper advertisement, Sewall House collection, Island Falls, Me.
33. H.C. Merriam, Letter dated September 18, 1907, Sewall House collection, Island Falls, Me.
34. "Sewall Gets a Frock Coat," *New York Times* (February 12, 1906), 1.
35. "Meddybemps Philosophy," *Boston Globe* (December 24, 1905), 20.

Czar of Aroostook County (pages 157–165)

1. Harriet H. Miller, *Mary Alice Sherman Sewall: A Biography Chinked with Fiction* (Island Falls, Me.: privately published, 1984), 63.
2. Miller, *Mary Alice Sherman Sewall*, 64.

3. Ibid.

4. Theodore Roosevelt, "My Debt to Maine," in *Maine: My State* (Lewiston: Maine Writers Research Club, 1919), 22.

5. William Wingate Sewall, *Bill Sewall's Story of T.R.* (N.Y. and London: Harper and Brothers, 1919), 111.

6. "'Bill' Sewall Is Appointed," *Boston Daily Globe* (December 17, 1905), 29.

7. Theodore Roosevelt, Letter dated December 26, 1903, Theodore Roosevelt Collection, Howard Gotlieb Archival Research Center, Boston Univ.

8. "'Bill' Sewall Is Appointed," 29.

9. "Smugglers of the Maine Boundary," *Boston Daily Globe* (December 11, 1904), SM4.

10. Miller, *Mary Alice Sherman Sewall*, 65–66.

11. Miller, *Mary Alice Sherman Sewall*, 65.

12. Miller, *Mary Alice Sherman Sewall*, 80.

13. Nina G. Sawyer, ed., *Island Falls, Maine: 1872–1972* (Island Falls, Me.: Island Falls Historical Soc., 1972), 112.

14. Miller, *Mary Alice Sherman Sewall*, 64.

15. Miller, *Mary Alice Sherman Sewall*, 73.

16. Sewall, *Bill Sewall's Story*, 112.

17. Theodore Roosevelt, Letter dated January 20, 1909, Theodore Roosevelt Collection, Howard Gotlieb Archival Research Center, Boston Univ.

18. Theodore Roosevelt, *Theodore Roosevelt: An Autobiography* (N.Y.: Macmillan, 1913), 323.

19. Roosevelt, *An Autobiography*, 324.

20. Miller, *Mary Alice Sherman Sewall*, 73.

21. Theodore Roosevelt, *Outdoor Pastimes of an American Hunter* (N.Y.: Charles Scribner's Sons, 1908), 412. Jonathan Rosen, *The Life of the Skies* (N.Y.: Farrar, Straus, and Giroux, 2008), 123.

22. *Proceedings of a Conference of Governors, May 13–15, 1908* (School of Law Library, Univ. of California, Los Angeles), 4.

23. Roosevelt, *An Autobiography*, 324.

24. Roosevelt, *An Autobiography*, 411.

25. *Annals of the American Academy of Political Science*, (1908), 9.

26. Roosevelt, *An Autobiography*, 447.

27. Jim Posewitz, "How the King's Deer became the People's Deer," *Delta Waterfowl Magazine* (Summer 2008).

28. Alden Stevens, "The Savior of Our Wilderness," *Sports Illustrated* (October 27, 1958). Reprinted from *Natural History* magazine.

29. Roosevelt, *An Autobiography*, 434–435.

30. Sewall, *Bill Sewall's Story*, 113.

31. Sewall, *Bill Sewall's Story*, 113–114.

32. Miller, *Mary Alice Sherman Sewall*, 73.

33. "Roosevelt to 'Bill' Sewall," *Boston Daily Globe* (July 16, 1908), 8.

34. "Roosevelt Honors His Tennis Cabinet," *New York Times* (March 2, 1909), 2.

35. Ibid.

The Passing of a Grand Old Man (pages 167–175)

1. Theodore Roosevelt, Letter dated December 19, 1911, Theodore Roosevelt Collection, Howard Gotlieb Archival Research Center, Boston Univ.

2. William Wingate Sewall, *Bill Sewall's Story of T.R.* (N.Y. and London: Harper and Brothers, 1919), 114.

3. "Roosevelt Thrown as Platform Falls," *New York Times* (March 24, 1912).
4. Theodore Roosevelt, Letter dated September 18, 1913, Island Falls Historical Soc. collection.
5. Theodore Roosevelt, *Through the Brazilian Wilderness* (N.Y.: Charles Scribner's Sons, 1914), 253.
6. Nathan Miller, *Theodore Roosevelt: A Life* (N.Y.: Harper Collins, 1994), 535.
7. Miller, *Theodore Roosevelt*, 538.
8. Harriet H. Miller, *Mary Alice Sherman Sewall: A Biography Chinked with Fiction* (Island Falls, Me.: privately published, 1984), 77.
9. Theodore Roosevelt, Letter dated March 8, 1918, Theodore Roosevelt Collection, Howard Gotlieb Archival Research Center, Boston Univ.
10. "Roosevelt Calls War Mismanaged," *New York Times* (March 29, 1918).
11. Miller, *Mary Alice Sherman Sewall*, 82.
12. Miller, *Mary Alice Sherman Sewall*, 83.
13. William S. Dutton, "The Big Woods Are Friendly If You Know 'Em Well Enough," *American Magazine* (1926), 54.
14. "Bill Sewall Visits Roosevelt's Grave," *New York Times* (March 24, 1919), 8.
15. Miller, *Mary Alice Sherman Sewall*, 86.
16. Ibid.
17. "Bill Sewall Visits Roosevelt's Grave."
18. Ibid.
19. Ibid.
20. "Bill Sewall Idol of Jersey Youths," *Houlton (Me.) Times* (May 4, 1921).
21. William Wingate Sewall, Letter dated February 15, 1921, Sewall House collection, Island Falls, Me.
22. "Bill Sewall Visits Roosevelt's Grave."
23. Miller, *Mary Alice Sherman Sewall*, 87.
24. Sewall, *Bill Sewall's Story*, 115.
25. William Wingate Sewall, Letter dated May 27, 1922, Sewall House collection, Island Falls, Me.
26. "Bill Sewall Visits Roosevelt's Grave."
27. Miller, *Mary Alice Sherman Sewall*, 92–93.
28. "The Passing of a Grand Old Man," *Bangor Daily News* (March 17, 1930).
29. Sewall, *Bill Sewall's Story*, 39.
30. Sewall, *Bill Sewall's Story*, 94–95.
31. Theodore Roosevelt, Letter dated April 7, 1887, Theodore Roosevelt Collection, Howard Gotlieb Archival Research Center, Boston Univ.
32. William Wingate Sewall, *Recollections of William Wingate Sewall of Island Falls Maine: 1845–1930* (Island Falls, Me.: privately published, 1972), 88.

Epilogue (pages 177–179)

1. Harriet H. Miller, *Mary Alice Sherman Sewall: A Biography Chinked with Fiction* (Island Falls, Me.: privately published, 1984), 94.
2. Ibid.
3. Miller, *Mary Alice Sherman Sewall*, p. 64.

Index